W9-CMB-399

6.75

GN
21
B38
H54

KABBARLI

By the Same Author

Descriptive

THE GREAT AUSTRALIAN LONELINESS (1937)
WATER INTO GOLD (1937)
AUSTRALIA, LAND OF CONTRASTS (1943)
FLYING DOCTOR CALLING (1947)
THE TERRITORY (1951)

Fiction

MY LOVE MUST WAIT: THE STORY OF MATTHEW FLINDERS (1941)

KABBARLI WITH ONE OF HER NATIVES

KABBARLI

A Personal Memoir of
Daisy Bates
by
Ernestine Hill

ANGUS AND ROBERTSON • PUBLISHERS

First published in 1973 by

ANGUS AND ROBERTSON (PUBLISHERS) PTY LTD
102 Glover Street, Cremorne, Sydney
2 Fisher Street, London
159 Boon Keng Road, Singapore
P.O. Box 1072, Makati MCC, Rizal, Philippines
107 Elizabeth Street, Melbourne
222 East Terrace, Adelaide
167 Queen Street, Brisbane

© *Ernestine Hill 1973*

This book is copyright. Apart from any fair dealing for
the purposes of private study, research, criticism or
review, as permitted under the Copyright Act, no part
may be reproduced by any process without written permission.
Inquiries should be addressed to the publishers.

National Library of Australia
card number and ISBN 0 207 12478 7

Registered in Australia for transmission by post as a book
PRINTED IN AUSTRALIA BY JOHN SANDS PTY. LTD. HALSTEAD PRESS DIVISION

One

BEFORE the image of Daisy Bates is cast in immortality, before the most remarkable woman in Australia's first two centuries is stylized into a Joan of Arc with visions and voices, or a Boadicea holding besieged tribal realms, or a Gertrude Bell of imperialist politics and policies, or a stained-glass missionary Mary Kingsley, as she will be at posterity's whim, it is a labour of love for me, after nearly twenty years of friendship, to keep the living memories, and draw in true colours the portrait the artists never painted in all her ninety years. The loss is theirs and ours.

Poets will sing her praises in odes and elegies, to rhyme with "Aborigines". Future Australians will meet her in infinite variety in films, novels, on the stage. Lady Casey, wife of an Australian Governor-General, has already written and produced an opera, *The Young Kabbarli*, with music by Margaret Sutherland, inspired by that dedicated life. A million or two of the rising generation in Australian schools will be "doing" Daisy Bates as a project, making a "social study" of her exile in the Stone Age with the last of the first men and women on earth.

She is a textbook and a thesis to be based on the records in our national archives and libraries, a "source" and a "course" in both the sciences and the arts, for anthropologists, ethnologists, historians, littérateurs and linguists. Memorials and plaques praise a famous woman in regions of Australia where once the little Dresden figure and the moving tent were a surprise in the primeval scene, a question mark. The smart little liner that boomerangs the west coast—Fremantle, all ports north to Darwin and back—sails in her honour: *Kabbarli*

For nearly a half-century that Aboriginal name was calling across the western half of the continent as that of a guide and a friend of the groups, clans and nations of the Old Australian, truly tribal, paleolithic people hidden away from the world on an island in unfrequented seas and for thousands of years miraculously preserved as a favoured race in their antiquity, but a rapidly vanishing race since the European invasion of a brief century or so.

A woman always alone, she followed the smoke signals of the oppressed and the dispossessed along three thousand miles of Indian Ocean coast, to places a thousand miles inland and a thousand miles apart—from the pearling seas north-west, down through the Hamersley and the Ophthalmia ranges, those old red crags and crowns now whittled away to multi-million tons of "iron, cold iron" and multimillion dollars in desert colonization, with centuries of steel in sight for international wealth.

She is remembered in the realms of gold . . . in the chequerboard of wheat and sheep . . . in the tall timber of the jarrah and karri forests, the glory glades of wildflowers and sea-coasts to the south . . . the ghostly white sandhills and cliffs of the Great Australian Bight, to the edge of grim nothing on Nullarbor Plain and the vast sandy deserts north-west. You can follow her pilgrimage and find her camps with the outcasts over another two thousand miles between the capital cities of Adelaide and Perth.

Hers was the aura of greatness even in her lifetime. She was always a world story, though lost and forgotten for years. To her own contemporary generations in Australia she was vaguely, too often scornfully, known as *"the woman who lives with the blacks"*.

No sane civilized woman could survive for a week the tribal life, the diet, habits and trials of the primitive full-blood Australian, much less the fastidious, sometimes finick-ing, Daisy May Bates. Conspicuous in the fashions of King Edward VII's day, exact and immaculate through all the drought and duststorms of the desiccating years, in the ulti-mate sandhills gloved, veiled, tailored, sailor-hatted, cravat-ted, shirt-waisted, voluminously skirted, bustled and trained, she was never in a blacks' camp except on her daily errands of mercy and research.

Her little white tent was always rigged a mile or two away, with a brush fence and a slip-rail where patiently they waited, never calling, never allowed inside. In gratefulness for her goodness to them, in awe of her dignity, but more in fear of her magic, none of them ever dared to intrude. The track between, the winding blackfellow pad through the bush, was soon worn deep in the print of their own splay feet and her little high heels.

When we tally the to-and-fro in miles of trudging, all the years of service in labour, in gifts, in loving-kindnesses, providing for an outcast human race in all its poverty and grime; when we remember the sameness and the silence of the everlasting plains, the torment of heat and flies, the bush tucker, the mostly milkless tea and butterless bread and jam; when we count the countless hours of collecting and collating from every region, every tribe, volumes of vocabularies, invaluable notes of every phase and facet of paleolithic lives; when we consider the recording by lamp-light, candle-light, fire-light, of knowledge old as the world, new to the world, written down in so many years of lonely nights: for her fidelity, courage, patience, and above all kindness, Daisy Bates is worthy of the brightest haloes we can find.

"Kabbarli kooj-iba! Old Woman different!" One of the Old Men, Gooinmurdo, said to me at Ooldea on the Transcontinental railway line where she spent nineteen years without relief among Australia's most primitive desert tribes, and where *Stone Woman Kabbarli* stands today in the faint shade of a mulga-tree. Freely, the phrase translates to "Old Woman, one only"—in other words, "None but herself can be her parallel." An anthropologist friend of mine, whom she dismissed with a haughty wave of the hand from her camp at Ooldea, insisted on interpreting *koojiba* as "crack-pot", but this I could firmly contradict from hearing south-central natives frequently use the word. Women and children of the Ooldea camp sometimes called her *Dhoogoor dhuga,* Loved One from the Dreaming.

Kabbarli, correctly pronounced Kahber-lee, not Ke-berley, means grandmother, Old Woman, in the old-time language of central-west coastal tribes of Western Australia: in their sorrowful exile to Dorre and Bernier islands near Shark Bay on the Tropic of Capricorn Mrs Bates was their gentle comfort and help. As Father Damien was to the lepers of Molokai, so was she to them, sharing their lives in those haunts of horror and death. The name *Kabbarli* implies wisdom and kindness, family love, understanding, authority

4

in the tribe. Aboriginal relationships are clearly defined and vital—Fathers, Mothers, Uncles, Brothers-by-skin, each with its duties, responsibilities, rights, and with the relationship names more usual in address than personal names. Mrs Bates carried *Kabbarli* with her through many tribes and languages in her pilgrimage from Broome to the Murray River, from 1899 to 1945. Gaining knowledge all the way—by which they were astounded and confounded—she was accepted by each successive tribe under that friendly name that showed appreciation for her remote and solitary life, her interest in their interests, her help unfailing.

She earned their trust and acceptance by her devotion in sacrifice and service and came to be revered as one of their own ancestral people, a pale spirit ages old to earth returning.

She was the only woman, white or black, ever admitted to their councils, to freedom of the totem as a full member of the tribe, the only one to attend and describe in detail the secret and sacred ceremonies and rites of their age-old phallic religion in its sacraments of circumcision, sub-incision, the blood-rites of brotherhood, vigils, ordeals, initiations and consecrations, with outward and visible sign in the Nine Ages of Man.

Most of her work in the early years was official, as protector, inspector, government representative giving out rations, assisting the missions, adviser in native affairs throughout Western Australia. She travelled all over the State to towns and stations to ensure that regulations for maintenance and employment were carried into effect, with distribution of food and clothing, provision for the aged, for children; and for the blind, diseased and afflicted at least some shelter and medical help. She then stayed at hotels in the little bush towns or arranged her own camps near a homestead rather than be indebted for hospitality.

Because she was fearless and truthful, no respecter of persons, by some of the townsfolk and station owners she was resented and ridiculed, as those in sympathy with the Dark Australians usually were. Because she was a crusader and critic of certain government policies, writing letters to the Press that fearlessly challenged some authorities, condemned injustices and cruelties—a voice crying in the wilderness for a truer understanding of an inarticulate race—by some she was called a fire-brand. Others said she was mad. *The woman who lives with the blacks.* Of this throughout her life she was scarcely conscious, and she was certainly not concerned. There was no room in her mind except for her own ideals.

As the work claimed her, her horizons widened to independent action and thought beyond the narrow racial confines of conversion and control—by Church and State. She travelled farther afield, far into western deserts to the truly tribal people still camped at their own hereditary waters in a way of life unchanged since the dawn of time. She was one of the first to find them not Neanderthal, half-ape, half-human, or war-whooping savages as the world then believed, but normal human beings, highly intelligent in their own environment and quick and lively in their comprehension of ours, with the same hopes and fears, laughter and tears, the same lovers, families, friends; she found them people of a merry and lovable nature, more submissive, more enduring. . . . She learnt to think with the Aboriginal mind. The white man's hatred and contempt sprang from lack of understanding.

She regarded them not as the Missing Link to be tamed and trained to perform, not as a charity fund or a duty, but as men, women and children in hunger and want, needing her care and guidance. She understood their abiding, engrossing, love of their tribal ground, their "country", every tree, every mound, where they were not nomads but pilgrims to the fertility shrines of their ancestors and the age-old nature gods and totems. In their unwritten histories and literatures, languages, laws, customs, folk-lore in fable, music and song; in the primitive arts and handicrafts passed down from father to son, from mother to daughter, through all the centuries, a new world of knowledge was unveiled for her alone. This was her field work, and the only way to achieve her goal was to share the lives of these people and become as one of themselves, but of a dual nature, with physical, mental and spiritual reserves.

She was a Woman of Destiny, and so she willed it. Once she had found her path—that winding blackfellow pad—she could never leave it. Forsaking all others, she gave her life this purpose to fulfil with a pitiful heart.

She came to the Stone Age to learn, giving in return. She was neither teacher, missionary, nor nurse, but all three as the need arose, both in the crude little crawl-in *goondees* of the wilderness and in the shambles of shacks and hovels on the outskirts of towns where the heirs of the first landlords of Australia, scavenging the white man's rubbish dumps, lived and died. All she owned, her personal income with all she could earn, was given to meet the needs of her people, to lighten their miseries, providing, defending, crusading, advising, explaining white man's law to the primitive, tribal law to the white, playing with the children, caring for the sick, comforting the dying.

Of her beloved Old People of the Stone Age she could see the end. For twenty-, thirty-thousand years their campfires, ever moving, had twinkled in the void of night, the only lights in Australia in orbit with the pilgrim stars; their strident voices had sung, in semitones falling and fading, the only human sound. Now all was changed and strange. In a hundred years in the eastern arc of the continent a thousand virile tribes from the mountains, the rivers and the plains, were gone and forgotten. Over and round and through the great western half-circle she followed the last of the campfires as they flickered out. Nobody else cared.

What manner of woman was she? I have often been asked. Was she the ministering angel or the martyr? Was she embittered, an escapist, an eccentric, a do-good crank? Why did she forsake Everywoman's needs and loves, home, family, provision, protection, household goods, the social and intellectual life in which she shone? Why did she forsake these for the homeless, shiftless wandering with the Untouchables, to be for ever estranged from her own loved ones?

How could a woman of her accomplishments and attainments endure the bush life in its long monotony of dusty oblivion, live in a tent through winter winds and summer torment of heat, drought, flies? Why the exile for years at a time without holidays, comforts, refreshment, with no companion or recreation to come home to at the close of day? Why was she alone in the work for over thirty years, independent of government assistance or public subscription, never asking, seldom accepting, a contribution even from her friends? Was she a Spartan, self sufficient with a will of iron, or a fanatic obsessed by a holy grail, messianic mission?

What did she do for the natives? She didn't teach them to earn a crust or to sing hymns and pray. She didn't teach them ambition, acquisition, application, how to gain citizen rights on award wages so that they could settle down in houses with hire purchase to pay their way.

What is the value of her scientific work, once derided by some scientists, now used as foundation knowledge of many Western Australian tribes of which no other trace or record can be found? Some scientists are apt to deride another's work if it does not bolster their own. Because she had no training in anthropology, no formula for correlating her scientific knowledge, her most valuable work is described by some as merely "humanitarian". Perhaps the word "science" with its demands for premises, analyses, and classification of facts found would not apply to the rapid and random jottings of all her days, her recording of knowledge as it came to light. Her real-life studies of the paleolithic mind, of laws, legends, literatures, and of the starry mythologies and eerie echo of long-forgotten songs, she gleaned for us from living lips in the gulfs of night and time, with her own world ten thousand years and two thousand miles away.

Anthropologists, university scholarships, and research grants were few and far between in her generation. Before Roth, Howitt, Baldwin Spencer, and Sir James Frazer in *The Golden Bough*, recognized the lost population of the fifth continent as a link in the migrations of primitive men, not a dozen people in the world gave them a thought as the proper study of mankind. Even today they are conspicuous by their absence from standard works and textbooks of world-wide authority in ethnological science.

Daisy Bates was not an anthropologist cut and dried to the pattern and the patois of today. She was a woman of classical and cosmopolitan education, an omnivorous reader, with a nodding acquaintance with French, German, Latin, Greek, with ancient and modern literatures, theologies, mythologies. She had a receptive and perceptive mind, a poetic imagination, a practical interest in the arts and industries, a quick

9

sense of humour and whimsy, a musical ear for phonetics, inflections and multi-lingual sounds, an insatiable zest for knowledge of all kinds. Nothing of interest passed her by unseen.

In the heat of the bush or in the smoke of campfires she scribbled her notes on the spot, in writing pads, on envelopes turned inside out, on rough scraps of wrapping paper when writing materials were not to be found. Odd rags and tatters of facts these might be, fables, genealogies, translations of corroborees and letter-stick maps, little dictionaries of the tribes, aboriginal songs and poems, jottings on customs, crafts, trade routes, with the hows, the wherefores and the whys. These miscellanies of memoranda were her reward; the jigsaw puzzle in faded ink and pencil, incomprehensible to anyone else, could be pieced together some day, she hoped, for a clear picture of native life and mind. As with all researches and collections, her notes became a fascination, a lifetime's work, enthralling. Sometimes she found a link in language, or a totemic kinship, or the end of a legend eight or ten years and a thousand miles from where it first came to light. The work was "humanitarian" indeed, undertaken to defend and protect the True Australians from the lie and libel that they were bestial half-men, "lower than the ape", not worthy to live.

Shall we think less of her scientific work, her knowledge drawn from the fountain head, because it was not presented in textbook form, and was pursued, without benefit of university salaries or government endowments or subsidies, by a woman alone in the Loneliness?

"To follow knowledge like a sinking star."

Daisy Bates had no intention of selling these treasures of antiquity for her own profit and advancement, though she well knew their value as archaeological archives. She

guarded them from moth and rust, floods and bushfires, a chancy and perishable burden for camels, carts and
luggers, in storms on land and sea. Towards the end of her
life they were her only possession—to be classified and
clarified as a gift to the nation, to Australia.

All else she had given to the natives, including her private
and personal income, her share in the profit and sale of a
pastoral property in Western Australia—allegedly sold for
£35,000—and the earnings from her literary and journalistic
work: articles, character sketches, stories, in free-lancing for
newspapers and magazines. Though eloquent and impressive
in speech, she was not a prolific writer. Haphazard publication at a penny and twopence a line in those years was not
very heartening. In the clamour and famine of World War I
and the financial depression that followed she and her
natives were quite forgotten. Literally sharing her daily
bread, she kept the camps going till 1935, when she returned
to the cities, at the age of seventy-five years for assistance in the
writing of her life story and for the compiling, with secretarial help, of her hundredweight of manuscripts about the
Aborigines.

Ninety-four volumes of these she presented to the Commonwealth Government at Canberra, as a guide to future
legislation and a research foundation for future Australians.

Sixty of her ninety years were spent in Australia, which
became her own dearly beloved country, her home ground.
Even so, she was never typically Australian. She was
obsessed with the Victorian vista of a boundless, deathless
Empire on which the sun would never set. The well-spring of
all her sacrifice and devotion was to be found in the clichés of
England's greatness, in kind hearts and coronets, in the
White Man's Burden, in "Right or wrong, my country!"
and, above all, in her adoration of the divine right of kings.

Royal grace and favour were the mainspring of her ideals, the one reward she wished for through the arid years; and in strange ways and places she achieved and received her reward.

Though born in the south of Ireland, she was *plus royaliste que le roi*, identifying herself, but in all humility, with some five generations of the Royal Family.

As a small girl, at Balmoral, she curtsied to Queen Victoria; as a young lady, at Yarmouth, to Edward VII and Alexandra as Prince and Princess of Wales. For George V and Queen Mary, when Duke and Duchess of York on royal tour of Australia to declare the first Commonwealth Parliament in 1901, she arranged the Aboriginal corroboree that greeted them in Perth; and through fifty years of cyclones and sandstorms she clung to the cherished umbrella that H.R.H. picked up for her when she nervously dropped it in her presentation curtsy to him at the Government House levee. It was hallowed by royal hands.

Edward VIII as Prince of Wales, George VI as Duke of York with his Duchess, later the Queen Mother, and the Duke and Duchess of Gloucester, were all on her visitors' list for Ooldea, *at their own wish to visit her*. Alone in the wilderness, she received royal visitors with perfect protocol, arranged command performances with Aboriginal dancers, or with grave dignity suggested the appointment of a "King's Man" as ambassador to the Stone Age. She was but the precursor, the pathfinder and the deputy for the man who would fill this role.

To the young Princesses Elizabeth and Margaret and to their "heirs, executors and assigns" she longed to devote and dedicate future books about the Aborigines, and in their names to complete her pilgrimage of the circle of Australia.

Strangely enough, these had become her Dreaming—

Royalty and the Aborigines. I never heard her express a wish to return to England. She had no desire for patronage, though her C.B.E. was a radiant recompense, more than enough to sustain her till the next royal visit. She sincerely loved the natives, not as a study or an object for philanthropy, but as her children in need of a friend.

"*Meenya jang-ga bomunqut!*" "The smell of the white man is killing us!" She was the first to translate the hopeless and terrible cry against the doom of a civilization. During her lifetime she had seen the tragic history of the European occupation repeating itself over and over again.

"To make their passing easy," how often I have heard her say. "By the end of this century the truly tribal and totemic race of antiquity in Australia, the treasure destroyed and a trust betrayed, will be vanished from their native earth." She went back to her old haunts till she was eighty-five years old, and could not find them in the end.

World War II had gathered them into missions, camps and concentrations all over the continent. The old order was changing. Nothing of them was left, except in remotest regions a few waifs and strays, soon to be absorbed in the new age of oil search and mineral exploration, as in the eastern States a century ago.

Now their children, and their children's children, from the first to the ninth generation, are born to be shadows of white men, knowing nothing of "country" or "language", speaking English from birth. They learn Aboriginal songs and legends concocted by Europeans, they learn to be tradesmen and trainees in our industries and schools. They study Aboriginal art and the lives of their ancestors in museums. The deserted wurleys and their orphan waters know them no more.

With the last of the smoke signals on the far horizons—

B

13

that writing in the sky for twenty thousand years the only written story of Australia—their pilgrimage to the camp of their *Kabbarli* has ended.

So much for the plaster-cast of immortality, the Woman of the Dreaming. Now for the living Daisy Bates.

Two

Hᴏᴡ ᴡɪʟʟ authors and playwrights of the future, in opera, play or documentary, interpret Daisy Bates from the intricate filigree of her life story? The actress creating Daisy has a surprise packet of a part. This Woman of the Dreaming, plaster-cast of the tragedy queen, is also a jack-in-the-box of perpetual motion and emotion, of pride and humility, of quicksilver in her joy of living. A beauty, a wit and a mischief, with all the pretty vanities, gaieties and graces of a Fragonard, she also has the queenly dignity or pensive wisdom of an Augustus John. She is a puzzle of contradictions and complexities, ageless but dated, fearless but supersensitive, imperious, impetuous, extravagently generous to others, self-willed in self-denial, a rock of ages in fidelities, yet quick to change in moods: one moment frivolous, the next earnest in ethnology, or eloquent in folk-lore, or grave as a judge. Her Irish pride and wit at variance, she is independent to a fault, quick to take offence, easily prejudiced, withering in scorn, but always a model of "good form". She sets no value on money—"While there's some there's plenty", to be given away or shared; but in her rigid rectitude her "gentleman's agreement" is her bond. She is never an Amazon or a battle-axe for a cause, but superlatively feminine; she is conventional, yet a rebel, agin' the government to right a wrong, with deep human sympathy, with courage and patience and a warmly loving heart.

Few leading ladies will surpass in personality the one-and-only Daisy May. Once seen never forgotten. She was immediately recognized in the cities after an absence of twenty years or more. A bright particular star in constant orbit, even in the silent bush, she could hold court in a blacks' camp or in Federal Government House.

Five feet three and never more than a hundred pounds weight, or lightness, of her, she was never thin, but nicely rounded in the hour-glass fashions of her time, and she enjoyed the best of health and stamina. She attributed her well-being, with never a doctor for thirty years at a time, to her outdoor activity and frugal living—mainly brown bread and tea. She was a confirmed tea-drinker, from piccaninny daylight till night most of her life.

Her chief charm was her voice, gentle and low, with an Irish intonation but not a shadow of brogue. In the written word she rambled, with too much to say; but she was an orator born, and could have enlightened the English-speaking world in lecture tours. But through two great wars these could not be arranged. She was eighty-five years old when peace was declared ... too late.

Born in Ireland on 16th October 1859, she died in Adelaide on 4th April 1951. As she told it to me, I recall the sequence of her life.

In an old yeoman farmhouse of Glen Carrick, near the village of Ballychrine in Tipperary, three small O'Dwyer children were lovingly cared for in their earliest years by their Grandma Hunt. An absent father, a shadowy young mother: both died in 1864 when Daisy May was five, Kathleen two years older, brother Jim a curly-headed toddler of two or three.

Ireland was still and ever the distressful country of the Great Hunger, with hordes of the dispossessed roaming the roads in beggary, sleeping in the fields and under the hay-ricks and hedges in the rains, stealing the scarecrow's hat and coat, poaching the "praties", salmon and trout from the lakes and streams, apples from orchard trees, a little pig: a sorry lot of scamps and tramps, barefoot, in rags, hiding from the peelers, praying with the priests, crying big tears for their loved ones dead in the famine or lost for ever God Knows Where across the seas. They were a troublesome crew and hopeless, lazy and shiftless you could say, the men with their shillelaghs, the old women with their cutty pipes, "as poor as wood", but no harm in them at all, and they could be merry in their misery. The children would hear them singing in the night, dancing and clapping at the jigs and the "Come-All-Yez" around the shebeens in the haunted countryside to keep away the death of cold and the devils of brooding hate and despair and melancholy.

Daisy May was to remember them many a time and love them for old sake's sake when she devoted her life to a people strangely like them, "heathens black as the ace of spades," some called them.

Grandma Hunt, by the great peat fire in the long twilight of Ireland, told tales of the leprechauns and troop fairies living in the trees, of furry clurrichauns, of Omadhaun the Laughing Fool striking you down with thunder and light-ning, of shapes haunting graves and ghost lights leading you into bogs—no end of queer things: voices in the wind of good and evil, animal-men prowling in the woods, shrines of the Gaelic gods in the Standing Stones, weird monsters living in the rivers and pools and all the snakes of Ireland before Saint Patrick drove them back into the sea.

Grandma Hunt gave Daisy May her first lesson in natural and unnatural history and mythology. In the sunny mazes of the Australian bush, the crags and creeks of the old red ranges and bright starlight of the endless plains, the little girl of long ago would hear a mopoke calling, or watch a moving *moondoong* light or "hear tell" of a *woggul* or a *bunyip* in a folk-lore that was much the same. She was at home again among the Dark People in their Dreaming.

Hers was a happy childhood, learning to read, write and "cypher", playing "Ring o' Roses" and "Red Rover" at the dame school in the dell, singing the loved old hymns on Sunday in the ivied Church of England at Ballychrine. The Hunts and O'Dwyers were not Roman Catholics, but that made no difference to their friendships and their faiths—no bigotry, no strife. For politics they were too old and too young. The first sadness was when Grandma Hunt died and the old farm was sold. The children were parted and never again united. Kathleen and Jim were sent to their father's relatives in Dublin, Daisy to a friend of the rector, Mrs Goode, widow of a Dean of Ripon living in North Wales. At eight years old she began her travels, across the Irish Sea, seldom, if ever, to see her native land again; but the green and the rains of it, its gaieties and sorrows, scalawags and saints, poetry and wit, its sing-song cajoling voices and quaint sayings, were in her memory all through life. Good Mrs Goode taught her to be a little lady, "prunes and prisms", very precise, and to do the fanciest of fancywork by hand. A bookmark of blue satin ribbon embroidered *"God Is Love"*, eighty years faded, Daisy treasured always in her Bible.

18

It was at about this time, on holidays to Scotland, that she curtsied to Queen Victoria. A wicked little trespasser in pantalettes and kiss-curls from a neighbouring vicarage at Balmoral, she was exploring the castle grounds near the famous summerhouse when Majesty rounded the corner, eyebrows raised under the regal black bonnet to register surprise. Daisy quailed; but till she was ninety she loved to recall her court etiquette, her presence of mind. Lifting her skirt on frilly pants, she bobbed up and down to the ground while the Empress of India and Defender of the Faith stalked on and almost smiled. From that time onward "the fierce light that beats upon a throne" held Daisy starry-eyed.

Fate keeps on happening. Within a few years Sir Francis and Lady Outram and their romping family of six, girls and boys, found room for the lively and loveable child in their county home, and so into their busy and exciting lives. She shared English, French and German governesses with the girls as they travelled all over Europe, home for the season, dancing at the county balls and riding to hounds, presented at court to the Prince and Princess of Wales, back to the grand tour again. "The Outram girls", as she called them, were her dear friends by correspondence through most of the outback years. No doubt it was in London drawing-rooms and Continental travel that she acquired the graces and affectations, the fashions and femininities of *Lady Windermere's Fan*, also the *noblesse oblige*, the high ideals of Empire service and the secret yearning somehow, somewhere, to be another Florence Nightingale or Harriet Beecher Stowe, or both combined.

Meanwhile, being fierily independent, it was her intention to earn a living as a governess, a genteel profession for impecunious young persons, the Jane Eyres and Becky Sharps of popular romance. But with a decline in health and grave fears of what they then called "consumption" she was advised by the doctors to leave the long winter miseries of cold winds and clouded skies for the bright sun of Australia and the keen clean breath of eucalyptus over three million square miles. This was a frequent prescription for those who could afford it and sent thousands of emigrants to "the Colonies", some to spread the contagion till tuberculosis became a national menace in Australian cities for a while, and others, like Daisy, healthy ever after for ninety years and forgetting why they came.

She arrived in 1884, when she was twenty-five, with a sheaf of introductions, at first to Tasmania among the landed gentry of the Midlands and the north. In their manor houses in the hedged fields with avenues of oak and elm, the hawthorn lanes and apple orchards, the sheep knee-deep in clover and the shepherd with his crook by the brook, they had made Van Diemen's Land, with all its bitter memories, a younger, sunnier England.

The demure little governess-to-be had the time of her life, riding to hounds with the antipodean hunt clubs, going in buggies and drags to picnics, to the wildflower woods or the old stone mills with the water-wheels turning, singing in the church choir, dancing at the balls. Tasmania was one of her brightest memories, with all its well-known families of the north, and if she was ever a governess it was only part-time.

Years after we had written her book, *The Passing of the Aborigines*, I was assured in Launceston by some old friends of mine, whose mothers well remembered Daisy O'Dwyer, that she was "pretty as a picture and lively as a cricket", a tease and a "flirt" with the "eligibles" all round her, and gaily dancing all the dances—waltz, polka, mazurka, schottische and Lancers—while the home-grown beauties were ranged like hollyhocks along the wall. When she sailed away to the mainland they heaved a sigh of relief for their chances . . . and in their old age they were amazed to hear of her life-long sacrifice.

There were no Tasmanian Aborigines in the eighteen eighties. Truganini and William Lanne were dead, last man and woman of an Arcadian race in a paradisal island. Not even a sigh of remorse was heard for the swift and cruel genocide by massacre and banishment to a bleak and arid Bass Strait island. Their skulls, as curios, were sold to museums.

In Victoria and New South Wales, after a hundred years of persecutions and eradications, the natives were already detribalized and the full-bloods few and far between. In a camp at La Perouse the last of the Kerredai of Port Jackson might be seen; and in the country towns of the "interior" the scarecrow remnants, the outcasts whipped from their rivers and ranges to make way for the settlers' cattle and sheep, were begging round the houses for wood to chop for a meal, selling for clothes-props their ancestor-spirit trees, and selling their women and children to brutalities. The Black Wars, the Black Police in their iniquitous punitive raids forced by the white man to slaughter their own race, the gold rushes, fevers, epidemics, starvation, the damnation of drink and venereal disease—the same reign of terror stretched from Victoria to North Queensland. Charles Darwin had looked for the Aborigines in vain when he crossed the Blue Mountains in 1836. "Death has been busy here!" Charles Sturt regretted, returning to his Murray River within ten years of his discovery. In every district, every region of settlement or occupation, their "dispersal" was swift and sure. Daisy heard of them only as a treacherous pack of thieves and murderers.

New South Wales was not the Australia Felix Tasmania had been to Daisy. Sydney's large population was graded: there were noisome slums, tenements and terraces where people were crowded in beehive intensity, mansions for the establishment and the new-rich. In the "cow-cocky" country to north and south there was more of child slavery than education; westward, poverty-stricken pioneers in raw iron shacks with bags for blankets, lived on bread and treacle and their own salt mutton and goat. West from the rich pastures of the coast—manorial estates of the land-grant gentry— were the squatters and the big sheep stations round the drab little towns all the way to Bourke and Broken Hill. It was Henry Lawson's "country cursed for sheep", with his death-less army of sundowners and swagmen, the Toe-rag Brigade, plodding an endless roundabout for work. Trade unions were young, industrial troubles smouldered, and soon the Shearers' Strike erupted, a political civil war a thousand miles long, from the burning of the paddle-wheeler *Rodney* on the Darling to the siege of Hughenden in the Gulf—first victories in the crusades that made Australia the "working-man's paradise" it has become.

Mrs Bates travelled about the State like a dot of quick-silver, experiencing life, that was real and earnest, shouldering her share of the hard work of pioneering. Of these years few personal details were given. Perhaps she was more often a governess than a guest, but battling in the crusades, I am certain, making friends and a few enemies, being outspoken, devoted to children, lovingly impulsive. Here she met her husband, John Bates.

"John Bates was once head-stockman on Tinnenburra," a bushman said to me. "Any man who could rise to be a head stockman on Tinnenburra was like a Prime Minister to the West. To hold down that job would take him anywhere, and you could put it on his tombstone when he died. He was somebody." Tinnenburra, just over the Queensland border, was millionaire Jimmie Tyson's head station, famous for the biggest woolshed in the world, half a million sheep to a shearing "in the days of the red shirts and the blade shearers".

In Daisy's treasure-pack of photographs was one of John Bates, head and shoulders stiff as a poker, a good open face sun-tanned, a trim pair of manly moustaches. She would pass it by or turn it down with a mischievous smile. "Marry in haste . . ." she might say, or "Least said, my dear . . ." or "Long ago and far away. . . ."

One day, in a reminiscent roundabout, she told me how it came to pass:

"He was an admirable man," she said, "of the most generous nature and the highest integrity, an upright man in every way whom everyone respected, and a magnificent rider, don't you know? That was the great attraction for girls in those days, in the Colonies especially so . . . . and for the picnics and races and woolshed dances in New South Wales you must have a gallant escort because there were such long distances to go. Well, there was a gymkhana, a Wild West Show, with all kinds of races and prizes—high jumps, breaking in horses, wood chopping, drafting out sheep with those wonderful kelpie dogs, and rough riding a young bull, and those mad things that still go on but I think nowadays they call it a rodeo. To me it was most exciting because I was a stranger to all but the hunting-field and the steeplechases back at home. I was there with the squatters' wives and daughters from the stations and selections round about, such a crowd! And dressed up to the nines in our Dolly Vardens and bustles and bombazines, a fashion parade, you know. They'd made lashings of cakes and pies and sandwiches for luncheon under the trees with bright new buckets of billy tea you dipped your pannikin in, and it was great fun for man, woman and child.

"To see the show we sat on tiers of forms they'd built up in a sort of grandstand in a paddock for the showground, with brush hurdles and a circus ring and a winning post. Everyone knew everyone, the men sitting on the stockyard rails to shout and cheer, and surging to and fro, barracking for their own riders and their own run.

"Jack Bates was there. He was a great friend and favourite of the girls where I was staying. They were never tired of singing his praises to me; they thought the world of him. He was a bachelor too, with some of them out to catch him, I could see. I'd never met him but they pointed him out—a fine figure and handsome, I had to admit, in his wide-brimmed, wide-awake hat with white silk neckerchief, Crimea shirt, cummerbund and Canton moles, his high-heeled riding-boots polished so you'd see your face in them! He was heartily laughing and joking with everybody. They said he'd come in for the show with a big team of horses and horsemen to compete in various events, but he wouldn't be riding himself, he'd let the others win. He had far too high a reputation to enter the lists with the young jockey boys or against his own men. Also he was non-competitive, a member of the show committee.

"So he was out of the picture *until* . . . they brought in an outlaw for the buck-jumping, a wild, unbroken colt fresh from the brumby muster that nobody had ever ridden. It had a rough saddle half on and they offered a guinea a minute to anyone who would sit on the wicked thing. It wasn't really a colt but a great rangy red roan, old in villainy, with all the devilries, propping and prancing, rearing up on its hind legs and pawing the air, tossing the riders

24

onto the rails to break their backs, doubling and biting their heels, and rushing the stockyards to scrape them off on the rails and trample them. Oh, it was an ugly brute, a savage and a vicious stallion. Of those that crawled up on it as it waltzed and whirled like a windmill in a cyclone not one could sit it for the fraction of a minute. A couple were hurt and all of them badly thrown.

"We were nearly in hysterics and calling to let the thing go before it killed someone when Jack Bates strode into the ring. He ran about with it and belted it, tightened the girth and mounted, how I don't know; but he leapt into the saddle and thrashed it round in that little ring with it springing and hooping itself like a tiger, biting the dust then lifting with all four feet in the air and the rider sky-high hanging on by the reins and coming down crash in the saddle. It was dreadful to see, the ugly brute flecked with sweat and foam and its yellow teeth knashing, biting and fighting and trying to kill; but it couldn't get rid of him, and soon you could see it was lurching, failing, and he belted it round and round till it was weak as an old buggy horse, puffing and gone in the knees. Then he rode it to a standstill, vaulted down and threw the reins to one of his men, and to all the shouting and cheering and whistling and roaring he came forward with a grin. He held up his hand till there was silence.

" 'I didn't ride this nag for a guinea a minute,' he said; 'but reckon up the minutes and divide the prize with the boys who did. I was one of the jokers who brought this brumby in, and if I wasn't game to get on him myself I wouldn't be asking any of them. Right-o! On with the show!'

"At that the crowd was madly cheering. I said to my friends, 'I'll marry that man!' And I did. It was that day we met and we used to go riding and racing together. Sometimes he rode that red roan brumby that he'd broken in, and it was quiet as a lamb. We danced together at the woolshed dances, and it wasn't very long before he asked me to marry him . . . and I did."

Eyes bright and cheeks pink with excitement, with no shade of regret, Daisy polished her dewy spectacles with a dainty lace handkerchief she had taken out of her belt. With a judicious glance for the far past she finished her story—

"A fine man!" she said. "A good man in every way, and a superb rider! But I never could run in double harness, don't you know?" A mischievous little smile.

All who remember her will agree: she could not live in captivity. The only feasible husband I could have suggested for her was a Viceroy of India where, in a benign autocracy with the divine right of kings, she would have been an omniscient, omnipotent, all-loving and beloved vice-reine.

She married John Bates in Bathurst, a bride side-saddle in a riding habit with a little bowler hat instead of a wreath and veil and a drover's wedding with all the pack-bells ringing and a brownie for the wedding cake. And so to a drover's brief honeymoon. Then back to the mob for the groom, to the sheep within the fences or along the roads, or to the cattle in the great unfenced beyond. Most brides stayed in the nearest towns or at their station homes for men must work and women wait in those days back o' Bourke. It was a year or so after the marriage that Arnold was born, their only child.

"The Drover's Wife", "Water Them Geraniums", "No Place for a Woman"—Henry Lawson has drawn for us in sad, drab colours the ordeal of women's days in the west of New South Wales, the highlights of tragedy in the lonely nights when they were still strangers to the bush, before they became Australians and found colour and beauty in an "opal-hearted country", and felt at home within the horizons of those wide and vacant plains.

We can understand that to Daisy Bates, dutiful wife to John, marriage became an impediment, a frustration, a subjugation of her temperament and will. He must be so often away, leaving her to endure those days far from the friends and interests she had known. Pastoral workers, stockmen, even overseers on the stations, until appointed as managers at the homestead, had never been able till recently to offer a wife a home. Daisy's marriage must have seemed an anticlimax to her education, her aspiration, a sad awakening from her girlish dreams. The wagon hitched to a star had taken a sudden fall; she found herself dependent, auxiliary, anonymous. They were saving for a home of their own, perhaps a selection, but on very limited means. Sydney or the Bush? A room with a baby in a city lodging-house, or oblivion in a dull country town?

Child-bearing, child-rearing, women's work that is never done: the radiant future was receding. Still a devoted wife and a doting mother, she brought the little boy with her to visit friends, joined in their social and benevolent interests, and began to hope again.

Even then, through her introductions and her good works she was a welcome guest at every Government House. In the photograph pile was one of Arnold, a large and chubby child of two years' old with sausage curls, tricked out in a capacious woollen suit of red-white-and-blue with gold buttons and military tabs, knitted for him by the Countess of Jersey when she was Governor's Lady in New South Wales. Cherished by Daisy till Arnold was a captain in the first A.I.F., it then travelled on for years as reach-me-downs to young hopefuls of the Great Sandy Desert, the last strands of it finishing up at Eucla as head-bands and corroboree gear for the Old Men and witch-doctors, *kunk-hi* and *pinnaroo*. A magnificent tiger skin, perhaps sent as a wedding gift from a vice-regal friend in India, years later she sold in Perth with other household goods to be hand-outs of flour, tea and sugar, bright print dresses, blue shirts, billycans, to friends from the Ophthalmia Range down to the Porongorup.

But the life's work was still ten years ahead, round the world and back to Australia. Sister Kathleen was married. Brother Jim was dead. She longed for England once again before settling down. When Arnold was five or six years old she left him, well cared for, with his father's friends and relatives on the South Coast of New South Wales, and set off on the voyage home, a free voyage on a sailing ship that doubled Cape Horn. They listed her as a "stewardess" at peppercorn wages, and she kept a diary of an exciting story she never had time to write in after life. She had intended to be not more than a year in England.

On her arrival in London she hurried to the bank, to find nothing but a cable from John. All but three of the banks in Australia had closed their doors on the ruin of tens of thousands. The colonies were bankrupt, stocks and shares worthless, the land booms over. Their own personal savings were gone and without hope of recovery. Arnold was safe and sound, but no money could be sent to Daisy in London; she must fend for herself, find a job.

Taking the advice of a friend, she applied that day at the offices of W. T. Stead, the brilliant journalist and newspaper tycoon, editor-publisher of the far-famed *Review of Reviews* and other popular literary, political and philosophical week-lies and monthlies, with columns contributed by the most distinguished writers, statesmen, scientists, in the English-speaking world. By a slant of good luck a corner was found for Daisy, a junior job as a library assistant at only £1 a week, in those days sufficient to pay very modest bed and board, and with promise of increases. She could revel in the work and its window on the wide world.

W. T. Stead's *Review of Reviews* and his other publications of international affairs—all the way to *Borderland*, monthly journal of the Society for Psychical Research—were windows on two worlds, the known and unknown. The library shelves in Daisy's realm were an afterglow of the golden age in Europe, its scientists, social and industrial reformers, sages, poets and writers. Here were the master-minds of all nations, and the wonders, such as telegraphy and the Suez Canal, that were creating a new man. Archaeologists were excavating his image and his memories from Neanderthal caves and desert sands, unveiling the ages in a clamour of revelations, interpretations. New and old religions, with armies of apostles and disciples, were all for the first time in history unanimous in chanting their anthems of the Fatherhood of God the Brotherhood of Man. For the first time, the masses could read.

Those were the days when Britannia, happy and glorious, a benign conqueror, was ruling the waves, emancipating slaves, glowing brotherly love and benevolence to a globe dappled pink by her wide-world empire. Daisy rubbed shoulders with the great ones of her day—Polar explorers, Everest climbers, pro-consuls—pathfinders in expansion of empire and trade, in triumph of civilization around the Four Oceans and the Seven Seas. Altruists all, even the battle-scarred generals with their "thin red line" of heroes storming the heights and standing siege.

Knocking on the editor's door came the philanthropists Cecil Rhodes, Andrew Carnegie, Baroness Burdett-Coutts; novelists and writers with their masterpieces, Thomas Hardy,

c

29

George Moore, George Meredith; Africa's Rider Haggard, India's Kipling, Hall Caine the Manxman, Olive Schreiner from her "African Farm", Conan Doyle with Sherlock Holmes, Marie Corelli with "God's Good Man", the mystics and dreamers, Sir Oliver Lodge and the Spiritualists, Madame Blavatsky and Annie Besant of Theosophy, Mary Baker Eddy of Christian Science; the missionaries and martyrs, their name was legion, living and dying for their vocations and revelations.

The prim little person in the library, worshipped at the shrine of Britannia, birth and breeding. She was familiar with and contemptuous of the world of intelligentsia and the battle-cry of freedom: the Socialists and the Great Unwashed; the Sidney Webbs and the Fabians with their red-headed rebel Irishman, George Bernard Shaw, a poseur and nonsensical; the Suffragettes and their sufferings for women's rights. Rigidly conventional, she was an anachronism in more ways than one. Women in politics were to her as crowing hens, unsexed, like Amelia Bloomer riding a bicycle, a comic in pantaloons. From societies, guilds and leagues of all kinds she remained aloof throughout her life; but the waving banners of their crusades fanned her ambition to achieve in her own right. Havelock and Nicholson, she told me, redeeming the wretched millions of India through the British Raj, were her pattern and her inspiration. But where was her path?

Her work on the staff progressed to that of a reader, assisting the editor of *Borderland* in his monthly muster of "ghoulies and ghosties", seances, ectoplasms, Egyptian guides and ouija-boards, doppelgangers and poltergeists, shadowings and echoings from the spirit land. She was to find them all again in the half-world of prehistoric man, and the Irish in her could never resist an atom of belief.

Nearly five years went swiftly by in London. Meanwhile Australia had made a brilliant recovery, with gold discoveries all over the west, another land boom, a stock exchange with multi-millions invested, and a rush of immigrants to a population of five millions on the eve of the federation of six unwieldy colonies into a Commonwealth. Family finances were heartening, and natural love and affection brought Daisy home again, hoping with husband and son to take up a pastoral property of virgin lands with low rental and infinite promise in the far north-west.

As she was leaving London, her interest was awakened by an item in *The Times*, that finger-post to roads of destiny, pointing so many pathfinders across the world to Arctic and Antarctic snows, African rivers, Amazonian jungles. A letter alleged that in the north-west of Australia iniquitous cruelties and crimes were being inflicted on the natives by the gold rushes and the settlers: murders and massacres, slavery with whips and chains, degradations and brutalities, drink and disease.

These accusations were a sensation in missionary circles and stirred up native protection societies to swarms of angry bees. Indignant denials and assurances of protective legislation were cabled to London by John Forrest's government from the West, but not necessarily believed. Mrs Daisy Bates, in person, called on the editor of *The Times* and informed him she was now leaving for the distant scene. She offered to investigate the charges independently, impartially, truthfully, to report such outrages in detail, and to study the condition of the natives with a sincere regard for their well-being as subjects of the Queen.

Three

IN A LONG LIFE'S PILGRIMAGE this was the first step.
Once the course is charted the long arm of coincidence
very often appears as a signpost. A passenger on board
ship from Rome was Dean Martelli of the Roman Catholic
diocese of Bishop Matthew Gibney, prelate of Western
Australia with its islands adjacent, an orbit of a million
square miles.

The gentle old Italian priest and Mrs Bates were soon good
friends. While crossing the Indian Ocean he sketched for her
the seventy years of written history of the great State, the
amiable nature and intelligence of the Aborigines, their
character and customs, their sufferings since the invasion of
British settlers of all their waters and their hunting-grounds,
leaving them in beggary and exile. He told her of the
remarkably successful Benedictine mission of Dom Salvado
and his Spanish priests and friars at New Norcia, founded
in the eighteen forties ninety miles from Perth among the
wild bush tribes of Victoria Plains, and of the gallant but
fated endeavours since the eighteen eighties of a band of
Trappist fathers from Sept Fons in France at Beagle Bay,

two thousand miles north-west of Perth, among the wilder Kimberley tribes beyond the law of the land and life's necessities.

The conquest of the West was the same easy riding that all the rest of Australia had been, the pattern identical from the first firm hand-clasp, white chief to dark chief, heart to heart, trusty and well-beloved, true as steel for peace and prosperity, sealing the pact with a bundle of beads, combs, handkerchiefs, hand-mirrors, turkey red and pocket knives (guns at the ready in case, and in warning to bring down a bird); then the invader's flag gallantly flaunting in the breeze above the million square miles.

Next came the battles—of Pinjarra, of this and that, for some forty years, and two thousand miles north to the Flying Foam and La Grange, the thin red line of heroes against the cannibal hordes; famous victories of Snyders and Colts against the pointed wooden stick of spears, casualties three or four at the most to three or four hundred of the enemies, and an open season declared for all blacks. Those still alive were banished from the waters and the pastures to make room for the strangers' animals. Their submission was cowardice; their defence of their homes and wives treacheries, savageries; their killing in hunger of a bullock or sheep capital crimes. The noble settler, to defend his home, was allowed to shoot at sight.

With the march of colonization came the police and the punitive raids, the jails, the chains; men, women and children (all rated as imbeciles) kidnapped as slaves for stock and station labour and for the pearling ships on a thousand miles of coast. The average life of the naked divers down to twelve fathoms for pearl-shell was two years in the sea; but by the kidnappers the crews were steadily replaced with hundreds of blacks from far-north and far-inland tribes, hunted down

33

with horses and guns, lassooed, "assigned" as voluntary labour with a cross for signature, and sold to the stations and schooners for £5 each, dozens in a batch. Provision of food, control of his blacks, was in the master's hands. Some masters were humane; some were fiends; their punishments chains or the cat, a pistol to scare the divers down, a bullet for running away or swimming miles, to drown. As for food, in a land with no transport, no daily bread, the natives often enough fed the white strangers with their own sea foods and game, while they faded away and died from malnutrition.

This was the same sorrowful story of all the eastern colonies in their first century; but in the west and north of Australia, with no influx of white population, the natives' were the only human hands to give help and without them the settlers had no hope, often depending upon them for life itself. This they had realized in time.

So Dean Martelli could explain to Daisy, assuring her that the deliberate cruelties and crimes of the article in *The Times* were nearly all of the bad old days. Whips, chains, kidnapping, employment as divers on the pearling ships or as beasts of burden, were now forbidden. The writings of Western Australian explorers, from Sir George Grey to Sir John Forrest who held the natives in high esteem; the sympathies and visits of State governors, representing the Queen, to regions once impossibly remote; the crusades of Bishop Gibney in the north; but above all the court reports, the telegraph wire and the cable that made such cruelties known—these had changed the minds of the white people to pity if not love. Magistrates, police and protectors must enforce humane treatment under government regulations. No longer could a native be shot at sight for stealing a billy-can of flour from a prospector's tent or in hunger killing

34

a sheep. Settlers and prospectors needed their guidance and labour, and labour permits were cancelled if ill-treatment came to light. Some of the settlers and their children had a sincere affection for the natives, and conditions were better than ever they had been.

Even so, there was much of heartbreak and injustice, of starvation and epidemics in the camps; there were occasional punitive raids, private vendettas; and, with public apathy, a low birth-rate, a high death-rate, whole tribes vanished from their regions within a few years. There seemed very little hope for this dumb, driven race.

Mrs Bates was deeply touched. Her first impetus was loving-kindness: she must help feed the hungry, nurse the sick, keep some of the babies alive. When she left the ship at Fremantle she shouldered the white man's burden for the rest of her life. Her husband and son, Jack Bates and Arnold, a schoolboy, had already arrived in the West—Jack Bates droving in the Kimberleys, "looking at country" to take up a cattle-run and make a home for his wife.

Mindful of her commission with *The Times*, Daisy bought a horse and buggy and boarded "the old *Bularra*", a rough little coastal steamer of those days, plodding up and down five or six thousand miles five or six times a year, tying up to the rickety jetties a mile long in the big tides, tides rising and falling up to thirty-five feet twice a day, brimming the beaches and leaving the sands bare. From Northwest Cape the world was far away—Onslow, Cossack and Roeburne, Condon, Port Hedland, shabby but brave little coastal towns thrashed by the cyclones, stifling in the heat. Once a year donkey teams and camel-strings straggled in from the stations with wool for the lighters and barques lying offshore and, months on the way, they carried back the stores. In half a million square miles of spinifex on the ranges and plains the settlers were up to a hundred miles apart with their sheep and cattle by the rivers and wells. With a few roving sandal-wood-cutters, mining camps of the Pilbara with lone hatters left behind in the ebbing tides of gold, boundary-riders in their huts, here and there the pioneer women at the home-steads, this was the scant population in a glorious hinterland as yet unsurveyed. All had to make their own roads. Schooners and luggers of the pearling fleets, with Malay and Asian indentured labour, divers and crews, were scattered along a thousand miles of reefs. Broome was now their home-port in its heyday, a patch of the Far East in the roseate light of its pearls.

Daisy set out in her buggy from the shanty at Port Hed-land with its blue blankets and earth floors where the hermit crabs nibbled her toes. Circling the plains and ranges south and west to Roebourne, in six months she travelled eight hundred miles. "Nor-westers" remembered that she travelled with her husband plus a horse-tailer and cook, but these are not mentioned in her book. She could scarcely have travelled alone.

Every station had its camp of half-civilized blacks of vari-ous tribes and languages, "boys" and "gins" riding to the cattle-musters, branding, droving, or employed as shepherds and shearers, pumping at the wells, scouring the wool in the waterholes, stamping it down into bales, labouring in to the coast with the donkey-wagons and Afghan camel-teams to load it into the ships.

Lubras with spinifex brooms swept the houses, watered the gardens, milked the goats, or rode in the stock camps with the men. Old Chinamen, as a rule, were the station cooks. No wages were paid to the natives. They worked for their tucker—and clothing of sorts—and a half-stick of tobacco a week. By government regulation the very old and the very young of a camp or tribe must be maintained by the employer in return for the labour of the bread-winners they had lost.

Daisy saw the crippled and blind crawling in and out of the *goondees* low on the ground, or sitting all day in the ashes in hunger and rags, keening the songs of their countries, the tears from their rheumy eyes running down their deeply grooved cheeks. She saw them sharing their rags of clothes with each other, sharing their food with the dogs. She heard them singing in the evenings their wailful elegies, to the beat of the boomerangs and tins and the little music-sticks. They reminded her of her own people in Ireland when she was a child. Perhaps that was why she gave her life to them.

The usual picture of blacks' camps in all the stations and towns of the West, the Centre and the North of Australia till late in the nineteen thirties was a shrieking clamour of starving dogs and a human rubbish heap. Half-caste children were running with the blacks. A few of the stations were well-managed, the natives well-fed, with care of the children and medicine for the sick. At many an old homestead riddled with white ants the white settlers, lone battlers, forgotten men, were as poor and hungry as the blacks. "Pioneers, O pioneers!" The pitiful chapters of Australia's early history we must not forget. "The Lucky Country" was bought and paid for, God knows.

No cases of deliberate cruelty could Daisy report to the London *Times*. The bad old days were gone; but here was a sorry problem where only fools rush in. She longed for King Solomon's "understanding heart". Around the old settlements of Cossack and Roebourne and zones of Pilbara and Murchison gold she read the police records, listened to grim tales often callously told. She saw the town camps of

37

squalor and disease, haunt of derelict and drunken white men, of Asian crews of the pearling fleet and the camel camps. She saw the natives herded in the reeking cells of Roebourne jail, the vast stone pile that, like slaves of the Pyramids, they had built for their own punishment, working on the road in chains or prisoned in stone walls, wasting their lives away for five or ten years for killing a calf or a sheep.

Another tragedy was the fate of the half-caste child, mother Aboriginal, father Asiatic or European. Belonging to no definite race, family or tribe, it was often enough at this time destroyed at birth or abandoned by the woman. It might live on in misery, neglected and rejected in the camps. It was the sad condition of these keenly sensitive children, in an environment from which they could not hope to rise, that frightened Mrs Bates into an unreasoning prejudice against them, a serious flaw in the loving-kindness she showered on all about her throughout her life. Accusing them of a tendency to the lesser sins and vices, she refused to foster a half-caste in any of her camps. She asserted her influence with Aboriginal women and boasted that no half-breed child was ever conceived in her camps. She forbade them to consort with white men and scorned the fathers of half-castes, even those honourable men who acknowledged and loved their children by Aboriginal wives.

She was a century too late. Children of many nations in all States of the Commonwealth were already a prolific hybrid race, a significant race. After seven generations of assimilations, tribal and racial, we still call them "Aborigines" today. In 1900 it was a different story.

From the lost world of the north-west Daisy returned to Perth for the other side of the picture . . . to be a gay socialite at Federation festivities, to mourn for Queen Victoria in a city decked with royal purple and black, moving to the

Dead March in *Saul*, to replenish her wardrobe for the last time at the age of forty, and to grace the functions to welcome King George V and Queen Mary when they were Duke and Duchess of York. So old a friend of the Family was Daisy, having known their parents and grandmother, that at the Government House garden party, overcome with emotion when presented to His Highness, she made a profound curtsy and dropped her sunshade. By royal hands redeemed, it was thereafter held sacred through fifty years of merciless sun and blistering heat as "King George's umbrella".

But now the dedication and the life's work intervened. Of the natives of Western Australia she read everything she could find, precious little indeed; but the praises and perceptions of such men as Sir John Forrest, G. F. Moore, John Lort Stokes, George Grey, made up her mind. Remembering the tragedy of the north, the need of the natives and their griefs, she offered her services in all practical ways to Bishop Gibney, who told her of his desperate endeavours to retain the Trappist mission at Beagle Bay as a haven and sanctuary in Christianity for tribes of the Kimberley coast. The government was about to resume the lease—of the only native reserve at that time in the north-west. Their land would be lost to them for ever unless immediate improvements to the value of £5,000 were made, Bishop Gibney explained.

It was ten hazy years since the little band of sixteen evangelist monks and priests from Soligny-la-Trappe in France had landed at Beagle Bay, a hundred miles north of Roebuck Bay, before the schooners of the pearling fleet and cable-laying ships from Java made Broome a seaport in the sand. They came to a wilderness of few white settlers and numerous lively tribes of salt-water blacks, with those of

Kimberley rivers and ranges still being "recruited" by beach-combers and sold farther south.

"The poor little Trappists," as Daisy always called them, in their brown habits and sandals, telling their beads on the beaches, were soon lost to sight in a very strange land. The wild blacks were their only friends, bringing them fish, crabs, oysters, turtle-eggs from the bay, bringing berries, fruits and yams, helping them build their monastery of bark huts and bough shades by perpetual springs in six hundred thousand acres of paperbark swamps and "pindan" sands, and to build the first little chapel of claypan clay. Groups and families of affiliated tribes gathered round them—Nyool-Nyool of Beagle Bay, Lombadina of Cape Leveque, Koolara-boolo and Koalgurdi of beaches to the south, Pindanawonga of the desert. Spell-bound by the masses and the music, quick to learn the hymns and prayers, they were thrilled to be blessed and baptized.

The Australian Aborigines of all regions were very easily converted to Christianity in its varied doctrines and creeds. Rituals and symbols they could well understand. The Father, Son, and Holy Spirit, Trinity, the Immaculate Conception the sacred shrines and objects, the mysteries and mysticism and priestly power in benediction and ban, the sacramental ceremonies, meditations, purifications, effigies, and so much else, even to the curses with bell, book and candle, were almost identical with their own in the instinctive worship and wonder of creation superhuman and divine.

Strange it was for me at Beagle Bay to hear the *Miserere*, and *Kyrie eleison*, the nightly litanies of *Ora pro nobis* with the wailing chant of corroboree to the *Sanctus* bells and the ringing sticks: under those starry tropic skies the massed choirs of Christendom and prehistoric man.

But the Trappist fathers with their silences and their fastings, ragged and barefoot by the springs at Beagle Bay, were too far from Seven Fountains and their beloved France. Some were graveyard crosses by the chapel of grey clay. Some were called away. Only four were left in the bark humpies of monastery "cells", living on pumpkins and seed rice. They had lost everything but their faith. Moth and rust consumed their labours in the heat and the rains. White ants and black ants ate them out of house and home. Cyclones swept the harvest away and drowned the fishing smacks, leaving them marooned far from aid. Their quiet congregations were there and gone, hither and yon on walk-about. The Bishop was determined to bring them back to save their souls, their children and their tribal grounds. Nothing short of hard labour for all concerned could redeem the wreck of the mission by assets and improvements worth £5,000.

Away they went to the north, Daisy and Dean Martelli, with a lay-brother, a carpenter, gardener, storekeeper, stockman, stores, tools, corrugated iron, transhipped from the coastal steamer at Broome to the old pearling-schooner *Sree pas Sair*, once the yacht of Brooke Pasha of Sarawak, now owned by Roderiguez, a well-known Manilaman. Three days battling winds and tides to Beagle Bay, she dumped them there and sailed away. Every willing pair of hands was called to save the place. They gathered in the natives to build and rebuild, to fence and dig wells, to muster, brand and yard the cattle running wild, to head the springs into irrigation ditches to grow greens—cabbages, lettuces, seven-year beans—for the pearling fleet and Broome. Daisy rallied the women and girls to plant and water the gardens and the rice-field, to paint the shacks, to help in the kitchen and bakery, to milk the goats, to bring in sea-shells for lime and sandalwood to sell, and with simple needlework to make and mend. She cajoled them to work by singing and dancing, making it a game for them to play. Admiring her energy, they reclined in languid grace.

Again she was learning about them, their child-like eagerness to please, their lack of acquisitiveness, or ambition, their delight in music and dancing, in comicalities, their patience and submissiveness, their happy natures underlying the griefs. She began to study their administration within the tribe, and learnt of the remarkable allocation of authority and duty by a system of relationships, laws, councils, customs, of the pilgrimages according to the seasons, ensuring provision of water and food for the term of their natural lives, of the allocation of countries to the tribes, ensuring through ten thousand years of isolation the survival of the race.

Though not a Roman Catholic, she attended all religious ceremonies. There was mass in the morning, the Bishop in his vestments with glittering mitre assisted by dusky altar-boys with great black eyes, the devout congregation kneeling to pray, men wearing only a *naga*, chest and back covered with tribal weals and holes in their noses where nose-bones have been, madonna and child, a young mother in a towel and a sarong, a bouncing naked baby in her arms, a shrill old woman in a man's shirt and a holey felt hat who brings with her a coolamon with prime cuts of carpet snake smelling to heaven and black with flies, an aged, aged man, white-haired and toddling beside his child-wife, no more than twelve years old; a hunter with a handful of spears and round his neck a medal of Our Lady.

In five months of manual labour the mission was saved. Daisy was known to all as *Kallauer*, Sister. Her gay and diverting adventures, her picturesque memories, make one of the merriest chapters in *The Passing of the Aborigines*.

As one of the first white women to be seen in the region, or in a Trappist monastery—at which she was roguishly pleased —she led the way for a gallant little band of Irish nuns who arrived eight years later, Sisters of Saint John of God. With the Australian girls who have followed them since then, giving their lives to seven generations of pearling motley and children of the original Aboriginal tribes, their work is beyond praise. The little mud-brick chapel of old times at Beagle Bay is now a noble pile with a high altar of mother-of-pearl, in the episcopal see of Broome, with a bishop of its own and a dusky congregation of New Old Australians rejoicing in peace, prosperity and all citizen rights.

The long arm of coincidence to Daisy was still signalling the way. Eighteen miles from Broome, across the claypans where the brolgas dance, is the cattle-run of Roebuck Plains. It was formed by Edward Streeter, a son of the firm of Hatton Garden jewellers that financed a pearling fleet in north-west Australia, their most distinguished shareholder Edward VII, then Prince of Wales. At the turn of the century John Bates was stationed at Roebuck Plains with his wife and young son, and here they bought the Hereford cattle to stock up a run of their own in the Ophthalmia Range, south-west of Marble Bar, across "bush blackfella" country and a patch of impenetrable desert, the Pardoo Sands.

Daisy was never domestic. Eight months resident at Roebuck Plains with a housekeeper in charge and a Japanese cook, she was free to ride with her husband in the mustering-camps. Daintily habited, side-saddle, her riding-boots polished and tasselled, gauntlet gloves, a fly-veil and a smart little bowler hat, she was mounting on a well-groomed hack. They carried a tent with luxuries of pillows and sheets for the track. There was heated water for the daily bath.

A "double-bed swag" was always a joke with the drovers,

and a "missus who cracked the stockwhip" was a standard figure of fun in some of the classic yarns of outback. Her kindness to animals, her politeness and passion for personal cleanliness—"a daily shave and a clean shirt for the ringers, and scented soap in the drinking-troughs!"—her anxieties in the midnight rush of the cattle, gave rise to a fund of anecdotes, kindly but amusing, that lasted them out for thirty years in a land where women were few and far between. Above all they resented her "anthropologizing", her unwomanly interest in "blackfella business", in the nightly yelling of corroborees and goings-on that no self-respecting white man, much less a lady, would be seen dead at. Some said she was "mad" from that time on. Little she cared, living, like Kilmeny, in the Dreaming, listening to its voices, learning its songs.

The Dinosaur's Track in the sandstone rocks at Willie Creek was an arrow, pointing her into the Stone Age. The fretted old effigies of Entrance Point, heads of the Pharaohs and Sphinxes staring out to turquoise seas, the red bluffs of Broome glowing coals in the sunset, trade winds, the big tides for ever whispering, sea-colours changing, the season of dense white mist, and high-piled clouds of the electric storms and the rains—all these were surely the stage-settings of drama and imaginings. She was nearer to the life, and minds, of the natives than she had been on the mission or in the towns.

Roebuck Bay was the stamping-ground of all the salt-water tribes of five hundred miles of Indian Ocean coast from Lagrange Bay north to Cape Leveque. In the serene beauty and leisure of a lavish land for ever summertime, with wealth of sea-foods and fertility of fruits, roots and game, its lively intelligent people, Koolarabooloo, entertained various neighbours all year round, even to the Pindan-a-wonga, far inland. There was always something doing, the Old Men's courts and councils, *Kobba-kobba* play corroborees, the turtle, salmon and other totem feasts and dances in their seasons, and *djoonbah*, the bush corroborees, initiations, the sequences of sacred rites and ceremonies in the Nine Ages of Man.

Daisy was amazed to find that the wanderfolk of the West still lived in their natural environment, in their pilgrimages, laws, customs, beliefs, memorized through their ten thousand years out of time. She saw the little patriarchal groups go by, the first gregarious division into families—the Old Adam with his stone axe on his shoulder, sons with their fishing net and spears, their wives and children hunters and gleaners from beach to beach, from oasis to oasis, still to be found within the borders of occupied country. She saw the groups merge into the clans, the tribes, the people of each particular region distinct and aloof from the others yet here affiliated and friendly at times, from necessity in a riverless patch of the coast. They "sat down" by the wells and soaks, amiable and active camps, busy night and day, the old ones happy to talk, like all old people. Among them were Daisy's friends from Beagle Bay, lovingly greeting her *Kallauer*, Sister, introducing her to the company.

She began by collecting vocabularies, "language", in which they delight, *wonga*, speech, a tribal possession of honour and pride. Of the boys and girls working around the homestead, always singing, she jotted down the little songs and sayings, their taboos and superstitions, children's games, a mother's crooning of a one-word lullaby and what it meant. The more she knew, the more they told her.

Hearing camp scandal, she learnt of the marriage laws and "skins", the food laws, the totems, relationships forbidden—that a lubra afraid to eat meat or silent for months was under a ban, that no man was allowed to speak with or even see his mother-in-law, even though he kept her in meat for years in payment for his wife. Riding the run with her husband, she noted the strange head-dress of a man, or the blister-weals on his chest and back in a design, women and girls with two joints missing from right-hand finger. She asked the reason why—tribal markings. "Him belong Sunday Island." On her morning walks she might meet a mother and her new-born child, pale as a white child, carried in the coolamon from last night's birth to rejoin the camp. Daisy would hear the story woman to woman, admire the little stranger with a gift or a name, and within a few days he was black as your hat to everyone's pride and delight.

She watched the "back-yard" industries of both men and women: the whittling of spearheads and stone knives; shelling and milling of samphire seeds; shaping and curving of boomerangs, spear boomerang, or the killer, or the comeback; carving and decorations of shields with glyptic writing of letter-sticks; the weaving of spinifex fishing-nets and sharpening shells and bones for hooks; the pointilliste art of pearlshells and stencil of bark baskets; the old and the crippled making string by rubbing possum or wallaby fur into a long thin strand on their thighs. Everyone in the camp would be doing something some time, not so lazy as they seemed. They told her the daily news from tracks on the sand or smokes in the sky . . . or she might follow a cloud of crows to a skeleton shrouded in paperbark like an Egyptian mummy, lying on a raised dais of branches between trees, reminding her of Bombay and the Parsees. Something to think about! A civilization!

She was awed to find a long-lost continent and its own people!

On the pindan plains of Roebuck Bay at twilight, to the cricket-clicking of the rhythm sticks, drone of a hollow smokewood pipe and the measured rattle of boomerangs— the world's first music of percussion and wind—*djoonbah* began. Whizz and whirr of the big bull-roarer, like the double-bass breathing of some huge animal, and the ventri- loquial clamour of men, beat as a pulse at the heart of the night all night long, fading in the tropic dawn.

In the old Streeter homestead, with its shell-grit paths and oleanders, Daisy listened and wondered. Nobody would explain. The white people laughed. They said "blackfella business". When she asked about it the stock-boys were silent, the house-lubras were scared. Visitors came from other stations, young boys among them, and all went *pink-hi*, walkabout, the women to *Jandu-ngunyal*, women's play- ground, Cable Beach, the men at campfires glittering round the bay from *Weeringan-marri*, the Standing Stones at Willie Creek, to *Thangool-ngunyal*, Bachelors' Walk.

The year's work with the cattle was over, the wet season was coming. White folk of the stations had travelled south for Christmas or into the town for "benders" as the case might be. The native population, with flour, tea and sugar rations as a foundation to bush tucker, was free. The men went hunting and fishing to provide the nightly feast and spent long hours of the day making up for corroboree with ochres and dyes from the seashore, cockatoo crests, erections of feathers and fibres, sticks and string, furry puff-balls, bones through the holes in their noses or puckering the upper-arm, sporrans of pearlshells and lizards' tails strung on hair-belts of human hair. Demon-masques and skeleton ribs, dot-and-dash geometries of squares, circles, triangles, all over bodies and faces, snakes, turtles, kangaroos, painted on their backs and moving as the muscles moved, were all of the totems. Every *goondee* was a theatre green-room of dressers and dancers bedecking one another or, more exactly, a vestry of priestly raiment and regalia while the producers, the artists, property-men—the "makers"—were busy with sun-ray head-dresses, peeled wands, the objects and effigies of altars sacred and profane. They sat in solemn silence daubing the new, restoring the old, in the grotesque *décor* of the antediluvian insignia and symbol.

Twilight of the Gods. Wagnerian opera festival at Bayreuth, with all its pilgrims, was never celebrated with a greater passion for perfection, a deeper religious fervour and dedication. But these age-old rites, never forgotten, were more than performances. They were sacraments of the oldest religion in the world.

Daisy discovered the women in their camps, faces smeared with fat and dust, with long paper wigs of hair for tearing in histrionic screaming and weeping—their part in the corroborees as sisters, mothers, cousins, aunts, to deliver the young boys to the uncle-fathers for the first initiations. Through all the various stages they may not see them again for a few years. They were out gathering *maia*, vegetable food, and baking piles of the cereal-seed dampers partaken of by the officiating "priests"—the unleavened bread of the Israelites, the propitiatory barley-cakes of antique Greece, perhaps the origin, in those most ancient times, of the Christian Eucharist! Her interest became profound, insatiable.

She was allowed to attend all the preliminary corroborees —as I myself have been in many regions of Australia, white women not being involved or in any way concerned. But Daisy undoubtedly stayed to observe the operations, mutilations, the vitally significant sequences and sacred ritual which she was one of the first to describe in detail at first hand. Walking for miles through the bush to track down that ventrilo-quial cacophany, sitting on a log for hours transcribing, trans-lating, inhaling the dust and din of pandemonium, the musky smell of black bodies glistening with sweat and grotesque as Goya's fantods, as Doré's devils out of Dante's hell, she has given the clearest and fullest exposition in detail of the man-making rites from childhood to age of the coastal tribes of West Kimberley, the most enthralling and authentic so far to be found.

She was, in fact, the only human being ever on earth to know the Australian Aboriginal from his conception in his mother's womb to the last shadow of memory on his grave in the tribal ground.

The knowledge she gained at Roebuck Bay she added to for forty years; she verified, varied and clarified the rites, customs, folk-lore of all tribes in the western half of the continent. The names here given to the nine degrees of initiation in the making of a man are those of languages of the north-west coast, where from *ngargalulla*, infant and child, to *taloorgurra*, Old Man, doctor of laws, sage, senator and Judge, she defined the education and described the inaugurations as first she saw them at Roebuck Plains.

Ngargalulla, the Dream-time children as in Maeterlinck's Kingdom of the Future, are spirit-children waiting to be born, or reborn. They must be dreamed and accepted by their fathers with symbols of their totem, country and tribe, before they come to their mothers at the "baby places", rock-holes, lily-pools, charmed places where the ancestors leave their seed for re-birth. The mother knows no other fathers. She had no conception of what we call "the facts of life", and not until the baby moved within her did she know she was with child. The little son or daughter is the child of the tribe, to be loved, laughed at and spoiled by all its "mothers" and "fathers" as a *ngargalul* until eight or nine years old, when sons become *nimma-nimma*, corresponding with our years of primary school. They ramble with uncles and fathers learning tracks, the habits of edible animals, birds and bees; they learn to hunt small game with their little boomerangs and spears and are taught the ethics of manhood in knowledge, ambition and pride. Their noses are pierced at this stage. Third is *balgai*, a coming of age. The boy graduates— to a high school, as it were, with first a grand tour of the tribal country with his guardians to greet friends and relations of all groups, inviting them to the great occasion, the most vitally important event in his life, *balleli*, the circumcision. Outward and visible signs of his probation and preparation are the possum fur band tied round his head and the knocking out of a front tooth, left or right, sometimes both according to custom of the tribe, first of the brotherhood rites. Then comes *balleli*. The child is now father of the man in the major rite of circumcision, practised throughout Australia by the second migration of the Aborigines, with so many other rites, laws, ways of life of the old Sumerian and Semitic people of the Babylonian Plain where many ethnologists maintain that human life began.

The boy is prepared by vigils and fasting, endurance of walking many weary miles, hearing the history of his Dreaming fathers, learning the commandments and the gospels of the totems as they are danced in corroboree night after night. In early years these ceremonies assembled up to a thousand in the congregations of associated tribes with four or five initiates from various regions, but to each is given the long rigmarole of spiritual training and saintly example mimed in the same corroborees repeated in detail over many thousands of years.

At the appointed time he is anointed with the oil of his

totem—emu or kangaroo fat, grease of the goanna, turtle, fish or seed soils—white-feathered and furred and ruffed, bedizened from face to feet in phallocrypt and cuneiform design of red ochre and white pipeclay, carried shoulder-high above the dancing, prancing debil-debil of daubed black men drumming in the dust. He is circumcised at *Barrangoolman*, the rise of the Morning Star. He lies on the backs of his elder brothers and "fathers" while the circumcision is made with a sacred stone knife by the surgeon-priest, the "doctor" of his group in the tribe. The boom of the big bullroarer drowns his cries, and the uproar of chanting the anthems and psalms of the Dark Ages, a chorale of men's voices in a religious frenzy, a mad elation in the mystery of Man and his divine power of creation, of the miracle trinity of body, mind and soul.

Night upon night the chanting dies in the distance as the *balleli* boy is left remote and alone, to live or die, to conquer fear, to endure hunger and thirst and find his own living from the foods and roots allowed . . . to brood on all he has learned of his phallic powers as the source of life, his debts and duties to his fathers in submission and self-denial, and, above all, avoidance of all women. He cannot see them. He is mesmerically blind, an exile.

Through the temptations of St Anthony, mortifications, the ban of silence, retreats and ordeals, his education in the marriage laws, the food laws, his degrees of initiation are attained by implicit obedience to the Old Men's Word. These degrees carry their own tests and trials, as our sports contests and university courses do, but they are purely spiritual, religious, more of the nature of Freemasonry with its Worshipful Brothers and Grand Masters. Might is not Right. Strength of the bully, skill of the hunter, the orator and the artist, have no power.

Brothers as one, the tribe as one—here is the secret of their centuries of survival.

Weerganju, the blood-pouring; *Jammun-ungur*, the blood-drinking, sacred rites of brotherhood for unity and loyalty, follow the circumcision, mingling of the blood. Each one carried its own stigmata. By his hair-dressing, his head-bands, his tribal markings, and by the scars of his dedications, multilations, his status of life is immediately known. His records and registrations, of totem and derivations, are hieroglyphed and cuneiformed in the sacred boards. *Kallee-gooroo*, the bullroarer, on his majority, he may wear in the chignon of his hair.

Through all these years without a wife, but earning a wife —like Jacob—by hunting for her family, he approaches full manhood at the possible age of thirty-five or so. As *maam-boongana*, eater of honey, he is entitled to an equal share with the Old Men of meat, fish, fruits, the best of the daily diet, and to marry the girl betrothed to him when she was a baby. As *taloorgurra*, he is an Old Man, himself, and with his hair flowing free a noble senator whose word is law.

Daisy, the sexless stranger at these secret phallic rites and blood-rites, describes them all in their interminable ritual detail in *The Passing of the Aborigines*. She was awed to learn that these poor old wanderers in their dingy rags, eating humble pie and owning nothing, walked like lords and philosophers in their private lives of the Dreaming, their age of fable in memories of evolution when birds, lizards, animals, were the fathers of men. She was amazed at the extravanganzas, the spectacles, dramas, oratorios, ballets, they conjured out of the red sand—fantasies of colour and mime, liturgies of forgotten languages, human mind and life before the creation of the gods.

But the wet season was over, and all the bush corroborees

of Roebuck Plains. Away went the stock-boys after the rains to general muster for the year's work with the cattle, Jack Bates and his ringers to cut out his mob for droving to his country in the Ophthalmia Range. Daisy was left at the homestead with the old folks and lubras in the station camp, making her first delightful collections of their songs and sayings, proverbs, superstitutions, legends and fairytales, lullabies and children's games.

Large as life in the heart of this fanciful world was Broome—in its crowded hour of glamorous life and romance, in the zenith of its mad, bad, glad old days, three hundred schooners and luggers scattered along the reefs in the alluring light of pearls. It was ten years old, a highly coloured picture-book of the East, population four or five thousand Chinese, Japanese, Filipinos, Malayans, Indonesians and their motley milling about in their Oriental villages of foreshore and mangrove creek camps and up to the bunga-lows of master pearlers, pearl-buyers from Paris, four hundred shell-openers out on the luggers, and the sahibs at the Cable House, Eastern Extension to Australia across the Timor Sea, coming up at Cable Beach.

Strangely enough, the pageant of pearling touched Mrs Bates only superficially. In that macabre history, that fateful industry, it was now forbidden to employ the aborigines, already her life's dominant interest. A woman of quick sym-pathies, she was never concerned for long with natives of other nationalities. She deplored the fact that the Asians inflicted the native camps with leprosy, yaws, the pox epidemics, malarial fevers, tuberculosis, measles—all of a frightening mortality with the prostitution of Aboriginal women and the syphilitic diseases: sins of the fathers, her chief reason for crusading against the increase of half-caste populations in the north of Australia as a national menace and tragedy at that time.

The Glen Garrick cattle, a mixed mob of breeders, 770 cows and calves, Herefords, the white-blazed "ball-ies", were out on the road—John Bates head drover with eight ringers —for the six months' circle of the Eighty Mile Beach, southward to Roeburn, east to Roy Hill across the Tablelands and the Pilbara goldfields, then climbing the rugged red ranges to Mount Newman and the head-waters of Ashburton and Fortescue rivers. Side-saddle behind them, neat as a trivet, Daisy May came riding with her dainty ways and precautions against sunburn, sunstroke, glare, sandy blight, prickly heat, stagnant waters, clouds of dust—Dorothy Vernon of Haddon Hall dehydrated on the raw red plains. From daybreak till nightfall they travelled a round thousand miles at a slow ten miles a day, her young son Arnold ringing the mob with the men or tailing the horses, following on with the spares. Her book keeps a graphic picture of the droving, with many adventures by the shallow wells and the few lone stations of the Eighty Mile Beach to Port Hedland, then wheeling south and south-east for the Hamersley Range and the Tablelands.

Many a night she unrolled her swag by a breakwind of saddles, by the campfire shared the drover's "scran" of johnnie cakes, tuckerbag beef and quart-pot tea, rode with Arnold the first watch to settle the cattle down, then washed away the dust of the day in a waterbag trickle behind trees, and under the starriest skies on earth slept to the music of pack-bells—the deep-tongued Condamine, crack-pot Kentucky, the small silvery tinkle of "Success to Horse Teams". She joined the midnight rush once or twice. Last off camp in the morning from meticulous ablutions and vanity-box precision of dozens of buttons, hooks and eyes, boot polish,

54

clothes-brush, nail files, hairpins, tiepins, veils, pigskin gloves, for lack of a groom-in-waiting she scaled the anthills to sidle into the saddle for a canter after the cattle and the cook's dray, falling in line with the "head drover", none other than Jack Bates, to run the show like a little queen. Some of the old bushmen still remember her, with smiles.

They thrashed the cattle up the ranges and swam them across rivers and creeks brimming from recent rains—Dale's Gorge, Wittenoom Gorge and Yampire, glorious scenery and today's mineral wealth in multi-millions then undreamed. Here the blacks wandered once upon a time in joyous freedom, but the gold rushes, the sheep and cattle settlers, and ruthless recruiters for the pearling fleets, had left only the old and the ailing in the few remaining camps. Daisy, in passing, listened to their legends and their memories, making notes on a pad kept in the saddle-bag, and pleased them with little gifts. Day after day in wishful thinking she tried to read the smoke signals to southward across the Maralanna plains with the help of the stock-camp boys. But cattle were now the mainspring of life. The mob increased to a thousand with newborn calves born on the trail trundled along in the dray.

Eighty miles from Roy Hill in a pocket of the ranges left with steep creeks that were soon dry gullies in drought, the drovers delivered the mob and rode away. Glen Carrick had come to pass, the new station property invisible to all but three Bateses. The first home was a bough shed with three rawhide sapling beds, nails in the mulga post for a wardrobe, a bush table and form, a kerosene lamp and kerosene cases for chairs. The kitchen was an outside fire with a camp oven under the ashes and three quartpots in the blaze. The cattle ran wild in two hundred thousand acres of red crags and yellow spinifex, in a million square miles of dust and glare in the Great Unfenced all round them. Better to travel hopefully than to arrive. . . .

A hell of heat in summer, this is the notorious Marble Bar region of Australia, temperatures over the century half the year, a world record of five months, without a day's break, of 105 degrees to 125 degrees in the shade. This is the country of the old bush joke that you can grill steak and fry eggs on the red-hot gibber stones. Flies, blowflies, mosquitoes, ants and white ants were a chronic torture. A perforated double-decker tin safe with a wet bag was a long way from refrigeration. For the milkless, butterless meals the menu was damper and jam, salted beef or goat. Mail and stores for the stations came by camel string pacing five hundred miles from Meekatharra, out on the Madman's Track three or four times a year, the bags of flour so long delayed they were often webs and mould.

The white man's burden in pioneering called for a cast-iron frame. White women were rare. The men, when their "hides were cracking", went in to the bush pubs at Marble Bar or Nullagine to add the scorpions, snakes and red-backed spiders of *delirium tremens* to the real ones already there. The mortality rate was high, "natural causes", sun-stroke and heat apoplexy, "the horrors" and suicide. Many suffered from sun-cancer and "Barcoo rot", a form of scurvy. It was a hard and dreary country, settlers about a hundred miles apart.

Daisy was not yet acclimatized to the poverty and the loneliness, the blank monotony of days, the long sleepless nights. She was worn thin by two tireless years in the north. After the wet they would build her a house—of creaking corrugated iron to beat the white ants. She had no desire to be a housewife, Mrs Station Owner, hard-working auxiliary to a hard-working man. Marriage was not enough. She was proudly independent and would have been restive as the wife of a millionaire. Her emotional needs as wife and mother were already fulfilled. Her childhood dreams of leading the leaderless, comforting the lost, on a national, an international scale, could be attained. She could see the way, and the sorrowful people to need her, and the joy in reward of expressing a human mind so young, so old, that it was new to the world—the Dreaming.

Her interest in the natives was resented as interference, her sympathies derided. Friction instead of friendship came her way, and she was ridiculed as "mad". Husband and son were embarrassed in their work among the men. Discussion became argument, tempers rising, resignation grew to desperation, molehills to mountains. . . .

With the threat of the big wet running the rivers and flooding the plains, cutting the roads to the ranges for three or four months, marooning the settlers without companionship or mails, without aid in illness she refused to be trapped. In a sudden impulse of righteous anger she left home in a thunderstorm with Arnold, returning him to boarding-school in Perth. They travelled in a buggy with a fossicker, Black Johnson, and a load of dynamite for his mine on the road to Port Hedland. Half-drowned for nine days in ten inches of rain, they bogged to the axles, climbed trees in swirling creeks, lived on bread and cold water, waded with the horse through an inland sea, not daring to leave the track.

From Hedland, in hurricane-time, they sailed south by the Singapore ship. There was no finality of separation but a parting of the ways. Jack Bates, of necessity, stayed with the cattle in the Ophthalmia Range. Arnold, at the Christian Brothers' College in Perth, where he was educated, became an accomplished pianist. Daisy returned to the world of thought and service, and to the natives, from this time on, her life and its desires were dedicated.

For a number of years they met, all three, at Bunbury for the Christmas holidays. They bought an allotment of land for a home looking down on the river at South Perth. . . .

The gulf of the years widened, too far for a bridge, Daisy following knowledge "like a sinking star" to the end.

Four

Jang-ga meenya bomung-gur!
The ghost smell is killing us!

A FEW MILES from Perth Town Hall in the rip and roar
of the freeways, along the Great Southern Railway
and highways to the south, you may still find the
Maamba Reserve in the lee of the wildflower hills where
the little white tent of Mrs Daisy Bates ballooned in the
breeze seventy years ago. Today its "Aboriginal" people
are greatly changed.

In the river-curve beyond her camp a queer little colony
of huts and shacks of wood and iron, kerosene tins, hessian
bags, crawling with dogs, black with flies, was the home of
the first landlords of Perth, a city mounted in gold, with
regions and realms of boundless wealth all over the south-
west. Thirty or forty poor old scavengers and comic cuts in
scarecrow rags, they begged round the houses, cut down the
trees to sell as clothes-props, ratted the rubbish dumps, sold
their women for a few shillings for drink, and died of malnutrition or the horrors. In Perth, as in every town of the

59

south-west, the death-roll was heavier every year, and few of the native children lived to grow up. Some of the Old Men in the various regions, as though in a cruel mockery, wore breast-plates of punctured tin proclaiming them kings —as they might have been in the other continents.

Last men and women of the Bibbulmun nation of south-west Australia, inheriting their paradisal lands for ten thousand years, they were numbered in thousands and prolific— *beebula*, many breasts—when the white men came among them at Swan River seventy years before, founders of the colony with Captain Stirling in 1828. In the handshake of faith and trust, their leader, Yalgunga, gave away the title deeds of all their realms for ever to the pale strangers whom they believed to be their once-beloved dead returning from Kurannup, the heaven across the sea.

Clans of the Bibbulmun, each of their own totem and tribal ground, were as close kindred as the counties of England or provinces of France. With the same laws and customs, language and way of life, they were of the earlier migration, uncircumcised, a man's initiation purely spiritual rites. From Geraldton south to Albany on King George's Sound and east to Esperance, from the sea-coast of rugged grandeur to the glorious hinterland, in tribal countries relatively small they were safe from famine and drought.

In spring and summer splendour of wildflowers they were sylphs and satyrs wandering in Arcady, a moving statuary among the woodland trees, laughter-lovers, music-lovers, spending golden days hunting in the hills or singing the nights away on the beaches. In the cold winter men and women wore the *booka* or cloak of kangaroo fur laced with sinews and sewn with sharpened bones, the classic garb of the forest primeval with all its flowery shrines that stirred the early French explorers to write of them as *"les beaux sauvages"* in poetry or prose. They were all friends and they had no enemies. So they had lived since time began in their own bright world—that was no longer theirs. Within the first century of settlement the last of them were gone. Descendants and motley to the fifth and sixth generations, quadroons and octoroons, are the "Aborigines" of Perth and the south today; but thanks to the patient years that Daisy spent among them in tireless service to all groups, translating their transcendent literature, we still can read their stories, hear their songs, and see creation in the dawn of time.

She was surely the first to render in English exquisite little Bibbulmun poems, voices in the wind—

> *Ngangar al den kal jeedamitch mokain,*
> *Warree warrong mooroort—mat yooar.*

> *Star falling, shaking and quivering*
> *Like fire spark ... relation of mine.*

A falling star was a sign of death coming to the *kalleep*, home fire. Or from Swan River where now the skyscrapers are—Bedeening, the Bugle Crane, stood in the shallows, and to Goonook, the Crayfish, he cried

> *Beelya, beelya, yeel-ai-ana!*
> *Moordinya, moordinya, noon-ai-anna!*

> *Soft one, soft one, come to me!*
> *Hard one, hard one, go away!*

Kardar, Long-tailed Goanna, was mother's brother and tribal father to Koolbaroo, Magpie. In winter Kardar went into the ground to sleep the cold away, and Koolbaroo looked for him everywhere, crying in his magpie music of chords—

E

Deero! Deero! Wonga le lannoy yalbing!
Deero! Deero! Wonga le lannoy yalbing!
Deero! Deero!

O dear, O dear! Speak from where you are hiding!
To Maamba reserve, as a haven from crowded roads and city streets, came all the old people of Swan River and the regions round it, as far south as Harvey, as far north as York, fifty of sixty homeless years behind them. Daisy was appointed by the John Forrest government as protector and a Justice of the Peace, commissioned to study the natives and to submit her recommendations for their well-being. She has sketched for us pitiful little pictures of the last of their tribes—Joobaitch, the son of Yalgunga who greeted the first white men, and Fannie Balbuk, last woman of the Kangaroo totem of Perth; Woolberr, a Black Swan man of Gin Gin; Mannop, the last Wild Dog man from New Norcia, Victoria Plains; a Snake from Kellerberrin, a Whitebait woman from Pinjarra, a Stumpy Goanna from Bruce Rock, an Emu from Wagin, and from Gnowangerup a Mallee-hen! She knew them by totem.

From these she acquired her Aboriginal mind, to be stocked and stored with Stone Age logic and folk-lore, languages and legends to the end, and they implicitly believed that she was one of them. After her day's work, care of the sick, doling out food and medicine, bailing out drunks from the lock-up, righting their wrongs, finding them jobs and in letters to the Press defending them, they would sit in the shade and tell her their tales, and sing—she with her pad on her knee, her busy pen snatching little treasures from oblivion. As old people will, they loved to talk of the happy past and their country, of how things came to be, their symbols, their credo and their measure of eternity. She realized their dual nature and value, human curios and human beings, and knew that the only way to understand them was to share their lives. Her mountainous collection of facts and fancies of the Bibbulmun alone, in her two years sojourn among them in all their zones and regions, light the way to anthropological science and establish the Australian as a link in the migrations of mankind.

Stories old as the world, new to the world, in long-forgotten languages, she translates and transcribes—stories of divinities and devils, of *woggul* snakes, benign and malignant, the spirits of waterholes; of Oracle Birds and Standing Stones; of the Creation of Man, his evolution through the totems; of a dark Prometheus bringing fire to earth, snatching a brand from the burning log of the Sun.

In her scattered volumes of notes, hastily taken, repeated in many versions from differen tribes and in different dialects, one is astounded to find new literatures unfold, unknown mythologies, undreamed philosophies, a Southern Hemisphere of thought, imageries of the world's first poets akin to those of earliest Egypt, ancient Greece. In her life of manual work and service self-imposed in the camps by day, with only the nights for writing in restless zeal, without comfort or ease, it is incredible the ground she covered, the field work she achieved, needing only compilation to perfect. Future students and writers about the Australian Aborigines will find her "ore at grass" ounces to the ton in nuggets and slugs and leaders to rich reefs.

She was one of the first to see that the Aboriginal soul and mind worshipped the same gods in different guise, conceived the same truths, according to their lights, as all mankind, evolved the same laws, shaped their lives to the same designs. The Aborigines believed the immortal soul of man existed before birth, beyond death, to live again. In the Bibbulmun heaven across the sea, a shore of sunset clouds, each group in its own tribal ground welcomed the loved ones to share eternity. After the pilgrimage on earth the *kaanya*, soul, must take the winding tribal road from the grave to the seashore, and travel under the sea with token, test, or fee to guide its way through pitfalls, snares, and enemies— some said a foaming weir half-way, some said the nest of Karruk, Black Cockatoo, the Pluto of the shades. He could send them back to be *kang-ga*, earth-bound ghosts, hated and feared, haunting to snatch the living away. If they passed the test or pleased him with their fee—a honey-bag perhaps, or a fish—he would let them go on to Kurannup and its happy campfires to live in plentitude and peace. Bad people and good, they said, all go the same way.

The golden-glowing *Nuytsia floribunda*, the white folk's "Christmas Tree", lighting the hills and valleys in December as grand finale to the pageant of wildflowers, was the Bibbulmun Tree of Souls, the *kaanya* tree on the winding road of the dead where the spirit rested on its way to the sea. A branch must never be broken, nor would the living camp near by. These trees are *winnaitch*, sanctuary. Woe betide you if you hear a whispering in the branches, or see a shadow in the shade. Swan River natives sang this song at their burial ceremonies:

> *Janga winjar!*
> *Janga winjar!*
>   *Ngobar weengar erunga.*
> *Ngalburdi waddai!*
>   *Nyoo! Nyoo! Nyoo! Nyoo!*

Spirit, leave us!
Let us alone!
Don't look back!
Go away over the sea!
Shoo! shoo! shoo!

They lit a little soul-fire and shifted the camp, sweeping their traces and tracks away.

But *jang-ga*, evil spirits, were everywhere, prowling in the bush to strangle and kill—in the guise of animals, birds, monsters and cannibals, running on all fours, in *dolya*, fog, in whirlwinds, *kjwadjardee*, in jack o' lantern lights at night. You could hear them laughing in the clouds on stormy nights, like Henrik Hudson's Dutchmen playing ninepins in the Catskills, shouting in thunder, throwing lightning spears, rattling their *kylees* in corroborees—

Nganya yoolagun, maiaga!
Murree kal boom! Murree kal boom!

I am on top in the clouds and can see you and
Hit your fire! Hit your fire!

All these are but one page of a thousand in Daisy's crazy pavements, her jigsaw puzzles of folk-lore and mythology in so many languages from different tribes, her random harvest of forty-five years. From every town and tribe in the south-west she enriched her Bibbulmun store of song and legend, totems and tribal dialects, life-masks and character sketches of these lovable and gentle Old Australians who had so lightly given away their birthright of the State's richest agricultural and pastoral lands. From Geraldton down across the sand-plains through dozens of affluent towns she travelled the rivers and ranges, the sea-coast of rugged grandeur, from Yanchep to Yalingup limestone caves, their bone-ghost skeletons filling the natives with horrors and fears—south through the wildflowers in their riot of splendour, close colonization of apple orchards, vineyards, wheat and sheep, stud farms, coal mines, timber mills, down to the jarrah and karri forests, Valley of the Giants, with some of the tallest trees in the world. She travelled west through realms of gold, feeding the hungry, cheering the lonely and the old, to the Land of the Qualup Bell on the shores of the Bight where Bibbulmun country ends. In the far south-west she was lovingly remembered by white settlers and natives. Daisy Summit in the Porongorups, highest peak in the ranges, was named in her honour. From here she made known to the world, in her writings then obscure but later to be remembered, the remarkable story of Aboriginal mateship, *Borung-gur*, the brotherhood rites.

It was during her term of teaching, assisting, supervising at the highly successful and revered Benedictine Mission at New Norcia that she weighed in the balance the values of Christianity in duty and doctrine and benefit, in regimentation of civilization, with colonization arranged and decreed in the white man's design for living. The miracle of Dom Salvado in bridging the centuries and raising the Stone Age on Victoria Plains to the Anno Domini of *homo mechanicus* was premature. His estimate of the wildwood population in 1845 when he came, an inspired young Spanish priest in the mantle of Saint Benedict from Norcia to Nyeergu spring in the wilderness, was all told 250 natives of the Wild Dog totem. Within a few years every one was baptized.

Fifty-five miles from the nearest town they had helped him to build the monastery and mission, floating the bullock teams over the rivers, night-watching the cattle, singing *Salve Regina* in a bog. Butchers, bakers, candlestick makers, cobblers, gardeners, shepherds, school-teachers, lay-preachers, he made of them all in a very short time, respectably married in streets of little stone houses, their women and girls good cooks and housewives, and all devout and pious . . . Jose, Scholastica, Carmencita, Pedrico, Juan, Marcella and Isabella, their children as altar-boys, telling their rosary beads, singing the masses in faultless Latin in the chapel choirs. Two of the Bibbulmun boys he had taken to Rome, first of the Aboriginal race to be received as monks, clothed in the Benedictine habit with the Pope's blessing, died on the way home.

Hundreds came to be christened and confirmed, all the surrounding groups and clans, and their children to school, quick to learn, to excel. Many could speak and write in Spanish, English and Bibbulmun languages. A Bibbulmun boy was church organist, while others played the 'cello and bass viola. Sportsmasters rejoiced in the first Aboriginal cricket team. New Norcia was thrice-blessed in all its undertakings, unique in Australia, an achievement known to the world when Bishop Salvado died in 1899, at Montserrat in Spain in his last years, leaving perpetual leases in faith, hope and love in missions throughout the State. The monastery is his monument, today a magnificent estate, a shrine, a retreat, a seminary, "All to the Honour and Glory of God" in its vineyards and olive trees. But its true Bibbulmun people have long vanished. Monnop died in 1910, his sister Beenaran in 1913—they were the last man and woman of Nyeergu, the Wild Dog totem of Victoria Plains.

Mrs Bates had observed that so it had always been with the missions and government compounds and institutions of Australia, where the full-blood tribal natives mingled with other tribes, losing, when sustained and restrained, their symbols and ceremonies, the freedom of their country, their bushcraft, their skill in hunting, their Aboriginal relationships and way of life. On many of the missions and reserves in their first generation they "sat down" in idleness and squalor, content to be provided for in subsidies and subscriptions from State and Church. Their daily lives were supervised, their work arranged, their names were changed, they lost their identity. Of their derivations and of their own people in the bush they were ashamed—"myalls, munjongs, nunga", simpletons, savages.

Ten thousand years behind world history and man's evolution, of normal intelligence and even intellect, they could take a spectacular step forward, but they could not catch up in one generation. They could be dutiful and amenable Christians, but with nothing like the intensity of fervour and faith that sustained the American-African negroes through all the cruelties of their slavery and exile. The negative Australian accepted the religion without emotion, endured the white man's authority without question, without protest, and of inanition obligingly died, without the will to live.

There were other, more obvious reasons why they failed to survive. To break up the marriage laws and certain "heathen" and primitive rites that seemed iniquitous to Christians, in many of the missions and reserves women and men, boys and girls, were herded into segregation, locked for the night in iron shacks with earth floors and barred windows, poorly ventilated in stifling heat, without sanitation or any knowledge of hygiene. Cleanliness of the wide bush, antiseptics of the sun and the eucalypt trees, were denied them. They shared each other's fevers and diseases—not the least, the evil eye of the strangers in the mission's mixture of tribes. Tuberculosis, venereal disease, eczemas, trachoma, in the north leprosy and yaws, were rife. Measles, diphtheria, typhus, gastritis, hepatitis, frequently swept through the camps and droves of natives died, even of common colds to which they had no resistance. Clothing was worn to

68

reeking rags, a source of infection. For the first half-century of "civilization" the decline in population with the infant mortality rate was so appalling it was believed in Australia that the Aboriginal women had secrets of birth control or practised abortion—when in shameful truth their babies were smothered or abandoned at birth in the mothers' fear of life. All over the State, as in the other States, Daisy had seen the rapid annihilation of the tribes by colonization and concentrations, as surely and swiftly killing them off as the notorious police patrols and punitive raids.

In the Victorian era of missionary zeal evangelists of every Christian creed were soon in the field, a Babel of European Languages, doctrines and dogmas, contradictory, bewildering to the native mind. In the north-west alone, in recent years, French, Spanish and Pallotine Roman Catholics, Anglican, Methodist, Presbyterian, Lutheran, even Latter Day Saints, Pentecostal and other denominations, in neighbouring colonies, claimed their congregations from the passer-by. It was difficult then to foresee that their abiding faith and perseverance, their care of the children, with education, brotherly love and the broader mind, would achieve the emancipation, the evolution of the full-blood tribal Aboriginal race—so long on the decline—into the virile and enlightened hybrid races of today: all over the continent, as in other continents, clamorous for their equality, freedom, and fraternity with the white. Since World War II they have travelled a long way, leaving the faith of their fathers far behind them and the prophecy to come true—that by the end of this twentieth century not one of the Old Australians, truly tribal, will survive. What of the future? We cannot fathom God's mysterious ways.

Daisy's legends people the earth and the skies. Her proverbs and parables from the twilight of fable, black magic in superstitions and spells, goblins and guardian angels, heraldry beasts and birds, Loch Ness monsters in Australian waterholes, antediluvian anthems and cantatas, even the lullabies and children's rhymes, in a folk-lore and zodiac strangely akin to our own, handed down in the spoken word alone through heaven knows how many generations, are only incidental to the life-masks and the profiles she portrays of living men and women of a now-forgotten race. These years were the most productive of her published writings and journalistic work. She contributed new and valuable ethnological studies to the government archives and to interstate scientific magazines, stories and sketches to the *Adelaide Register*, to the Perth *Western Mail*, occasionally to publications overseas.

As an example of her own writing in lighter mood, here is part of a character-sketch of Ngilgee, the last Busselton woman,—Ngilgee, a heavy-weight Helen in the Trojan wars of Maamba Reserve, a "hard case", high, wide and handsome, comic relief, the saving grace of laughter in that vale of tears—

"She was about sixty years old when the writer met her at the native reserve at the foot of the Darling Range in Perth, 1902. She had then thirty-two dogs, seven goats, a dozen fowls, four aboriginal suitors and a half-caste aspirant.

"A kindly understanding government during John Forrest's premiership had given her a plot of ground, fenced, for flower or vegetable growing, a hut, even a double bed and a spring mattress—for Ngilgee's dogs were her blankets at night, and thirty-two dogs and a hefty woman require a full-sized double bed.

"It was a weird sight in the early morning to see the living blanket wake to shrill noisiness—every breed of mongrel, mastiff, bull-terrier and Newfoundland down to a King Charles spaniel not a foot long, with only two working legs, half an eye and rickets.

"Ngilgee's favourite was *Yungar*, man. She made a little red coat for it as it hadn't a hair on its body. Its legs, fore and aft, were bowed like those of a successful jockey, its tail the exact resemblance of a pig's. It's flea-infested body was black and shiny. Its gait spelt "dog-rouéism" at its worst. Ngilgee fought their battles with them, and refused to believe evil of them. She "bulya'd" the policeman whenever he came to shoot them, and vanished with them to the ranges . . . then back they all came to set the settlers raging about their hen-roosts.

"In spite of dogs, goats, fowls, there were five suitors for Ngilgee's hand—Monnop, a Dingo man; Woolberr, a Black Swan; Bimba, a Turkey; Baaburgurt of the Salmon totem—all over sixty, two of them nearly blind, which didn't prevent them thrashing and bashing each other to win their dark lady. Ngilgee was very fair and kept an open mind till one day a half-caste, Jimmie, appeared on the Reserve. She threw Baaburgurt out with a bucket of cold water to take Jimmie in—but she reckoned without the suitors, who stood on guard, all four together, and beat him up whenever he came near.

"Ngilgee sang a lament for him—a soft minor musical chant with a haunting cadence. It told of a duel between the strong wild winds for soft rolling clouds—male for female. The cruel winds kept them apart as a boomerang tears the branches. The strongest wind must win.

"Nevertheless, Jimmie departed and was seen no more. When Monnop's jaw was broken and Bimba's ribs smashed in, both returned to their home ground where they died. Blind Woolberr, foot-walking home to Gin Gin for the

Black Swan nesting, was run over by a train. Baaburgurt died at Capel.

"Ngilgee remained. A favourite with Lord Forrest, who had known her since childhood, and who came to see her one day with the Governor and his lady, she charmed them all with her elegant manners and faultless English, which she explained. Born in a potato patch of some early Vasse settlers, she was abandoned by her mother in haste to avoid jail for stealing the potatoes. Passed on to Mr and Mrs Alfred Bussell of Busselton, she had learned dairy and house work attended school with the Bussell children till sixteen years old when she married her first husband, 'Whitey-Brown George'.

"A remarkable personality, she would come along the path to my camp on the Reserve, singing clearly and distinctly,

"Awake my soul, and with the sun,
The daily course of duty run.
Shake off dull sloth, and early rise
And make thy morning sacrifice.

"She taught her dogs to sing, to perform tricks, but the policeman won one day. When Ngilgee was out washing, he shot them all. A fine healthy woman and a hard worker, her life was long. Of the Kangaroo totem of Busselton, Ngilgee was the last lonely soul to find her way across the sea to Kurannup."

Five

Late, late in the evening Kilmeny came hame,
And naebody knew whaur Kilmeny had been.

THE PASSING OF THE ABORIGINES in its rapid survey of
so many years covers the ground with Daisy Bates in
her orbit of nearly a million square miles in Western
Australia and South Australia, the little white tent right
out of the world at times.

On the pilgrimage, in its places and persons unique for a
woman alone, her occasional fellow-travellers ranged from
the regals and vice-regals and Oxford and Cambridge dons
to *kurdaitcha* men—feather-foot!—ritual murderers of the
desert sands, trackless, anonymous, invisible, avengers and
executioners, human disguised as devil, wreaking capital
punishment for Aboriginal capital crimes.

As the years went on and her aloneness in the silent bush in-
tensified, speaking native languages for months at a time, she
began to think in the Aboriginal minds, in their judgments,
reserving her own, but never condoning their savageries and
violence, their evil magics of hate in sorcery, "singing" and

"boning", or their involvement in any wrong-doing against the white man's laws. As a Justice of the Peace, with a copy of the Statutes, sometimes she held a little court of her own, but more often to magistrate or judge defended, interpreted and explained the prisoner in the dock, wild-haired and dumb.

Across Gage Roads from Fremantle to Rottnest Island —now isle of holiday delights but then of misery and gloom, a native prison where offenders from all over the State were entombed—she was a frequent visitor, a Prisoner's Aid Society of one. Murdering myalls were there in gangs, no longer "hanged by the neck" at the scene of the crime as a gruesome example but in life imprisonment for obeying tribal laws. Cattle and sheep killers—when whipped from their hunting grounds and hungry—came from the Kimberleys three thousand miles away, "cheeky blackfellas out of hand" in defending their waters and their women in the gold rushes, or running away from the stations, or threatening with their spears the man with the gun. For the brutal killing of white men none escaped, whatever the provocation. As a rule, until 1930, the whole tribe was destroyed, and some of the neighbours, in a punitive raid to teach them a lesson.

Of seven or eight hundred prisoners at a time in Rottnest Jail from Supreme Court sentences of hard labour for five or ten years, not half of them lived to return to their country. Five and six to a cell in dark stone walls, navvying round the island in chains, these children of the sun, far from their campfires, died of "cold sick, homesick, poison" magic, in the long bitter winters shivered away their lives. A few of them tried to swim fourteen miles of turbulent seas to the mainland, and drowned.

Daisy was a friend, sometimes the only one in months,

74

speaking their language, bringing news of their countries, small comforts in tobacco or sweets—little could be done in jail routine. Sometimes she spent hours in a cell to cheer a dying man.

In her unending crusades she made no accusations of deliberate cruelty against white authority, the police or the settlers, most of them well-meaning and humane. She pleaded for understanding. She explained. She tried to kindle an interest, affection for the race, amusement as for a child and lenience in their failings, which she herself exaggerated at times. As she grew older she was learning from their sorrows the patience and forbearance of a pitiful heart, the pity akin to love. She could not leave them again.

At Dorre and Bernier islands, across the bay from Carnarvon on the Tropic of Capricorn, she was honoured and deeply touched when the blind, the halt and the maimed, poorest and saddest old wrecks on earth, waiting for death in exile, claimed her as one of their own.

In the language of the central-west, half a continent wide, in its zone from the Murchison River to the Musgrave Range, they called her Kabbarli, Grandmother—good, kind, wise Old Woman. She valued that as highly as her C.B.E. to the end of her long life.

Dorre and Bernier islands were a waste of shame, the cruellest mistake a well-meaning government ever made. From the recommendations of a noted anthropologist, the derelicts of all the tribes, the unemployed and unemployable on account of their afflictions and their age, left behind to starve when their breadwinners and hunters, the physically-fit, were taken away to work on the stations and the gold-mining towns—were gathered in by the police from north and south and the whole of the vast interior, sea-coast tribes and desert, the young ones afflicted but mostly the old. They were freighted in carts to Carnarvon and shipped across Shark Bay in the holds of lighters and luggers to the two barren and desolate islands north of Dirk Hartog, the men to Bernier, women to Dorre. Between them was a narrow strait with tide-rips impassable. Husbands and wives were divided for the first time in their nomad lives among feared and hated strangers from other tribes in ghastly camps of the crippled and the blind, the leprous and the syphilitic insane.

The well-equipped hospital with doctor, matron and staff on Dorre Island had cost the government philadelphian thousands, with transport and upkeep of natives, their food, clothing and medical supplies in weekly deliveries from the mainland since 1904. It was paying for death in exile and unutterable anguish—far more graves than people, death a release. For the living, hospital treatment was daily torture of "needles", doses, dressings, forcible feedings, enemas— they were chained to keep them from running away.

In a coma of misery and pain they spent their days, crawling in and out of their wurleys in the windblown sands or staring for hours across the tide-rip between the islands, making futile "finger-yabber" signs for their "boys" and "old women", wailing the nights away with their dreary keening to the click of the little sticks like heart-beats failing when the fires burned down.

Daisy, in 1910, arrived with the Cambridge Research Expedition and stayed for nearly a year, travelling with them backwards and forwards to the main, telling the news of their countries, giving the dying the courage to die in peace and, with the few who returned, seeing them safely home. She learnt more "language" and acquired the new accomplishment, in a small way, of cuneiform writing. Sitting with them while they carved *millee-millee*, letter-stick, send a message to each other or the family. She could read the dot-

76

and-dash cipher of a walkabout to or from a waterhole, the
wavy lines, the circles, rough hieroglyphs of the totems and
so on—a few glyptic signs to say "Trusting you are well as
this leaves me at present" or some simple message that a
child may write. She delivered the letter-sticks to and fro
between the islands, to their delight. The saddest memories
of her life were of those wind-swept isles of woe where she
became Kabbarli. In 1911 the Molokai was mercifully
vacated. "Cockeyed Bobs" and *willee-willees* have long ago
blown all its griefs and graves away.

Kabbarli set out on a pilgrimage of the central west,
through stations and towns of the Pilbara, Murchison and
Eastern Goldfields, a thousand mines but the high tides of
gold on the wane. Giving out blankets and government
rations, here, too, the Woman of the Sorrows found many
tragic stories, wrongs to be righted, dwindling of native
populations before the white. The Last of the First were
fading out of life. Only a few remained, on the edge of the
towns or on walkabout. As their tribal grounds were
deserted and their orphan waters for ever lost, they brought
her their sacred boards to guard or to deliver to their
successors in the councils when they died. They brought her
rain-stones of gold-streaked quartz and talluride and the
greased and ochred oval god-stones giving her right and
title to their countries, making her heiress apparent of
infinite pastoral and mineral wealth, but even for them that
was a comedy.

She was happier when an old, old doctor of Aboriginal
laws in the Weld Range, when dying, and in a secret con-
clave, gave her his *bambooroo*, a light curve of acacia wood
smoothly rounded, tapering blunt at the ends, finely carved
in Indian filigree winding and twining round a central
female figure suggesting the Hindu deities rather than

Australian *mourra* and totemic art. It was old in the Dreaming, he assured her, full of power or poison, good or evil, hot magic, "sun sitting down inside it", for blessing or curses, worn in the hair with white fur as a top-knot in the wild orgy corroborees, carried as insignia of authority, a Great Seal, as it were, for the ambassadors between tribes, commercial travellers in trade and barter, invitation to the rites. An anthropological curio of unique significance, as such it was written up in scientific paper. Daisy, as heir to its magic, found it invaluable in keeping order in the camps, at Ooldea quelling a rebellion. The form of engraving convinced her that India was a country of sojourn, if not of origin, of the second Asian migration of Australian Aborigines.

In seven or eight thousand miles of travelling, within two years the tent flitted like a white butterfly all over the central west, through the red ranges and eroded old breakaways like ruined castles across the yellow spinifex plains. It rested by reaches of the rivers, rigged between the ghost gums and reflected in silver with the golden banksia blossom and the scarlet of desert pea. It folded and unfolded by soaks in sandy creeks and wallaby warrens, on the outer rim of mining towns with the big mines still going, poppet-head spires and batteries, in the nuggety gullies by this time deserted and by the salt lakes mirrored in mirage. The lone camper had no interest in stocks and shares or in ingots of gold, no desire for material gain or comfort. Neighbouring towns and stations were friends in her need, and she was always independent, the monthly mailman calling with her mail and stores.

Her care of the natives was sometimes derided but never seriously resented because she was completely free of ulterior motives or politics in any degree, never for, with or against

78

any party and actuated only by her own exalted ideals of Empire unity and the divine right of kings. Strikes, demonstrations and trade unionism rampant she looked upon as sedition and "ugly". Self-pity, recrimination, bitterness and vindictiveness were far from the truly Aboriginal nature. Sadly enough, they endured their misery in a mute resignation with very little resistance or retaliation—they asked but little here below.

She was perfectly safe among them through the decades of lonely nights, even when out of sight and earshot of the mining camps and settlers, and among the uncivilized, who never will leave their campfires for fear of the debil-debil in the dark.

But the white woman has always been a being apart in the Aboriginal mind, having no place in their marriage laws and relationships. They suffered no sense of inferiority in the white man's foreign and complicated world. They never wanted the things he craved, they envied him very little except his tucker when they were starved. There was therefore no desire to possess, to rape, to humiliate or to murder his woman in revenge or jealously, although for his crimes against *their* women or defiance of their laws often enough the white man paid with his life. They welcomed white women at the stations, and as a rule were generous, helpful, harmless, loving the white children as they loved their own —nobody kills Santa Claus. Pioneer women all over Australia were at home alone in the homesteads for months at a time when the men were out with the cattle many miles away on the run, the blacks' camp full of defenders should the need arise. On the rare occasions in history when white women were murdered by the Aborigines—the notorious Hornetbank massacre in Queensland and that of the brig *Maria* on the Coorong, South Australia, and one or two others here and there—it was usually in a clean sweep of a family in blood lust by a gang or an attack on strangers by the uncivilized.

From Marble Bar and Nullagine southward through Meekatharra, Cue, Mount Magnet, eastward to Wiluna, through Menzies, Leonora, Morgans and Malcolm to Laverton, south again to Kalgoorlie, Norseman, and through all the great mines in the litany of gold, Daisy came driving her buggy along the roads of the camel teams, donkey-wagons, coaches of Cobb and Co. Her work was always sadly the same, to temper the winds of winter to the indigent and the old with her beef tea and blankets, "coughin' medicines", healing ointments, cleansing soap, simple cures and little comforts, government rations and warm clothes. These poor desert primitives rewarded her with knowledge new to the world and many thousands of years old, birth, death and fertility rites, variants of languages and legends, sometimes an innocent indictment of the white man in their clouded and allegorical truths. At Laverton she found a "lice totem" group in the degradations of the camps, at Yalgoo the "blood totem", where all of a tribe died of tuberculous haemorrhage within a very few years, the spitting of blood their fatal symbol.

Forty-five miles west of Cue in breakaway country of the Weld Range they made her a shareholder in Australia's oldest mine—the remarkable hill of Barlooweerie, its present name Wiljiemia, "red ochre's home". An isolated hill in the Weld Range, four hundred feet high, twenty-six million tons of decomposed haematite ores in probably the richest deposits of iron ore in the world, it glows with the sacred red ochre pitted and seamed with blackfellow pads, with ridges and ravines, shafts and drives of constant and primitive mining through timeless ages, the ochre, *doo-arree* or *wiljie*, bartered far and wide, used in all industries and ceremonies, chief article of Aboriginal commerce throughout the continent, a source of great wealth to the local tribe. The scene is wild and eerie, a frowning range with half-shapes of outcrops and great boulders in red loam plains. These are the *moondung*, sleeping—the gods that guard the place.

The open cut on the crest of the hill is fifty feet across, eighty feet deep, pockets and tunnels from all levels winding in mazes deeper still to stopes and galleries like the Pharaoh's tombs in the Pyramids. The walls within are crumbling dust of rust, the tracks worn deep by the bare feet of countless generations and flanked by the ashes of little fires to clammy clay vaults the colour of blood or a livid mauve. Many thousands of tons have been excavated since the far past with a diorite hammer and a wooden drill, the ritual tools of the task in the hands of paleolithic miners, then carried for miles in wooden scoops and bags of bark, to be left at the borders of country and traded to neighbouring tribes by unseen salesmen, in payment for what they required, a fair exchange. No thief or invader ever tried to jump the claim, to the native richer than gold. Invasion and appropriation were unknown in Australia until 1970. Strange devils guarded strange country, serpents and monsters lurked in the waterholes. Kabbarli was no stranger. She must take her *bambooroo* as visa, she was schooled in the manner of approach.

Wiljiemia sentries were the *moondung* Meeril, Illeeree, Doogulgoora, great boulders guarded in their sleep by Daabidgee, the *woggul* of Dhan-ga-noo waterhole near by. There Daisy Bates must camp for the night in silence, no singing or dancing to wake the *moondung* or a *wheenyu*, whirlwind, would gather about her and she would die. Taking a green branch she must follow the winding path to

Meeril, on the crest, then down into the mine descending by little mounds of stones to mark the way and the ashes of fires. Here and there crawling through a tunnel she was dyed red with the clay. Silently, quickly, taking the ochre in her wooden scoop, she must walk backwards coming out, sweeping away her tracks with the green branch. From the top of the hill she must run for her life lest the *moondung* stand up to kill in thunder and lightning. . . . The rich little pocket of red ochre belongs to the stranger now, and the *moondung* are forgotten long ago.

Sermons in stones, history books in the waterholes of prehistoric man, still lying down to drink with his lips to the pool. . . . As ever, her pilgrimage of graves, the white woman a mourner in strange rites. . . .

The margin faded as she slipped away from the realms of gold towards the shores of the Great Australian Bight, *Dhoogoor Yuara*, Road of the Dreaming. In the Arctic-white sandhills of the south coast, in the blinding glare of Nullarbor Plain and the honeycomb of its limestone caves in a thousand miles of so called "waterless waste" she was to find a twilight of the gods, the same old remnants of Aboriginal tribes "sitting down" in their last camps, women and men, for her to comfort and befriend.

On a little ship from Fremantle that still battled round the Leeuwin on a thousand miles' voyage to deserted ports of the gold rush days along the south coast, she pitched her tent for a year or two at Israelite Bay, Twilight Cove, Eucla on the border, farthest east in Western Australia. Leaving the Bibbulmun at Esperance she found tribes distinct and different, fresh fields for research. The Kauera at Israelite Bay were strongly Semitic, not only in cast of countenance but in racial traits and customs, circumcision again, Mosaic laws and Old Testament legends such as the Flood and its one surviving hill-top group with totem birds and animals of an Aboriginal Noah . . . and of Aaron's rod striking a rock for water . . . and "Incarnate devil in a talking snake". Hebraic patriarchs with flowing locks and headbands, Hebraic profiles and curled beards, had much impressed the pioneer Dempsters who named the place.

Mulba, minning, nunga—men—languages changed but Aboriginal life was just the same, in these riverless sands the restless walkabout to the rock-holes and shallow wells unending, to the wallaby warrens and the wombat-towns in good seasons. In rainless years they licked the heavy dew from the saltbush in the early mornings, standing the roots of the water-mallee in their wooden scoops to drip and drain, digging for the little yellow frogs distended with water deep down in the clay, sometimes entombed for years. They could weather a famishing drought on ants' eggs, mulga apples, cork-tree flowers, lizards, edible fungus, where there was no game. To the north was no-man's-land, Nullarbor Plain, the treeless void of never a track, never a sound but the howling of devils in the wind from its caverns and blow-holes where Jeedarra the Python lay gigantically coiled.

As the other countries of other continents excelled in their own arts, skills, accomplishments, graces, beyond the essentials of living—writers, philosophers, sculptors, musicians, painters—so in Australia, explorers in bark canoes, song-and-dance men, the carving of stone tools, fur and feather craft, murals on cliffs. Those of the south coast were the star-gazers.

Daisy Bates, in a unique line of research, was to find and translate a new mythology of the Southern Hemisphere, close kindred to the Greek and in imagery and in allegory related to all others. She was to find totemic signs of a second zodiac in the moving planets and fixed stars, deities of earth now in heaven, all the camps and countries, cult-heroes and tribes on perpetual walkabout in the map of the night skies. Out of the silence she has saved for us the visions seen, the stories told around the campfires of the Stone Age to a thousand generations, setting down in her written word snatches of songs from the first singers on earth.

Aboriginal astronomical beliefs and legends are treasure trove hard to "dig" in the Aboriginal mind, as I found in my own search for them among innumerable tribes. No more than an occasional flash in the pan came my way, in a study that calls for patient years among them as one of themselves. There may be a thousand miles between beginning and end of a legend, or several different versions in a few hundred miles. One facet only may shine, the name of an animal or bird, a friend, or a foe, no one remembers why.

At Williambi, Twilight Cove, Mrs Bates found *Wonnunda*, the Tree that Reaches from Earth to Heaven—Yggdrasil in myths of the Norsemen a world away. The Wardunda and Kalaiji people said that long ago in the Dreaming, when birds and animals were men, the *mulba* could travel up and down, but Native Cat *Ginnega* and Ant-eater *Winoin*, man and wife, stole the heavenly fire and burnt down the tree. Digging a hole in the sea to hide the fire, by the Sparrow-hawk *Mer Mer* and Blue Pigeon *Karrgain* they were seen. So as not to scare Ginnega with shadows, they flew higher to see. Then Mer Mer crept down with his spear, Karrgain with her digging-stick, throwing the fire from the sea to the shore for the *mulba* to find and warm themselves and cook their meat for ever. *Karrgain* is the spirit of every campfire—Blue Pigeon feathers you can see curling up in the smoke, and the women sing her song when they light a fire—

Karrgain gulainba
Nam Bal! Nam Bal!
Ilambala gin gin,
Ilambala gin gin!

Karrgain flying
Higher! Higher!
Till no shadow falls,
No shadow falls!

Walja-jinna, the Eaglehawk's Track, is the Southern Cross, Eaglehawk *Walja* highest of all and lord of the skies, the Pointers *Dhurding*, his waddy near by . . . *Warroo-boordina*, fire-carrier, Black Cockatoo with red tail-feather is Antares to us, and Vega, *Gibbera*, Turkey, burnt his feet with the fire and the nails dropped out and fell at Wilyinagabbi as *kandi*, stone knives. Altair is *Kaanga* the Crow, Aquarius *Bailgoo* the Brush Fence. Rigel is *Kara*, Red-backed Spider, in Orion's right foot, Magellan's Clouds *Murguru*, *Oimbu*, Right-handed Brother, Left-handed Brother, who take the souls of the dead. Never point at Magellan's Clouds, the Two Brothers, *Boolbarradu*. *Kallaia*, Emu, is the Great Black Bird in the Milky Way, Road of the Dreaming, *Dhoogoor Yuara*, but to some tribes the River That Never Dries. Legends and fancies among these neighbouring tribes of south-central desert and coasts are nearly as many and as varied as the stars, *Kata*, Heads, the Planets on their nightly pilgrimage to the heavenly waterholes. Banded Goanna *Milbarli*, Kangaroo Rat *Wailburdi*, Red-backed Robin *Joombin* with his wife, *Minning-Minning*, are there in the constellations with Aquila *Kaanga-Noonju*, Crow Mother, Delphinus *Kaanga-wandi*, Crow boys, Canopus *Jurr-Jurr* the Night Owl, Pisces *Warramula*, Kurdaitcha men on the trail.

85

Corona Borealis was *Kammin-gammin* or *Juin-Juin*, Babblers, the "baby birds", once a hunting-party of men sitting under a tree with their crack-pot laughter, leaving babies there for the women to find—

Juin-wongain, wongain, wongain
Jokers talking, talking, talking.

Half a mile from Eucla, the noble old telegraph town now engulfed in the ghostly white sandhills, Kabbarli rigged her tent between the Karduing salt-water people and the Yalgura, of Central Deserts around Boundary Dam. "Capital" of the south coast, on the South Australian border, Eucla was founded by Sir Charles Todd in Overland Telegraph No. 2, transmitting news of the world from the cable in Western Australia, a jetty with ships calling, streets of fine stone houses, a grand old station comfortable and cool, a concert hall, a racecourse, and home from home for forty telegraphists of South and West Australia, night and day ticking away in Wheatstone, "talking, talking, talking" like the *juin-juin*. But in 1912 Eucla was already deserted for the Balladonia station and the telegraph line direct to Coolgardie gold. The population in Daisy's time was an old English gentleman, Chichester Beadon, left behind as caretaker and for two or three years forgotten among the empty houses and the graves. He was first to cross Nullarbor Plain from south to north, to put in time. His salary cheque and Daisy's mail came from Albany on the three-monthly boat or by Mick Allan, a wild Irishman and "the South Coast Poet", driving his camels three hundred miles round the shores of the Bight in six days. Settlers a hundred miles apart had only the roads they made—a lonely land.

So far Mrs Bates had enjoyed government sponsorship,

provision of rations, expense account. Over the border she was left to her own resources. Her gentle suggestions to the South Australian government that she might be made a protector, a provider, a Justice of the Peace as in Western Australia, were scarcely heard—she was too far out. For love of the work, the mesmeric power of the great wide spaces of Australia and its True Australian people, she decided to sell her share in the station, the home at South Perth, her few cherished possessions and pictures, books, jewellery, even a tiger skin rug that a Viceroy had sent her—still remembered by friends of hers in Perth. She became a busy free-lancer to the *Register*, Adelaide, the *Western Mail*, *The Children's Encyclopaedia* of Arthur Mee in London and a few other publications; but as a long-distance, two-pence-a-liner by candle-light in the silence after the day's toil and travel it was not heartening work. Her virtue of loving-kindness was its own reward. Delights in discovery were hers— parables, proverbs, signs and omens, scraps of history and natural history, abracadabra of magic, of medicine, the mind of man in its first consciousness and comprehensions of a universe.

At Eucla she found Venus! The evening star in all its brilliance hung low over the pale shallow sea and luminous white sandhills to be *Yeergilia—Yugarilya*—the beautiful woman, heartless, beguiling, who eats her lovers, kills the young boys in their retreats, leads astray the children. The white people had shortened her name to Eucla, as white people with Aboriginal words ever will, but none of them knew her—elder sister of the Pleiades. These were the Mingaree girls of Aboriginal myth, totem of the little desert dragon, for all his corny humps and curious colours, gentle and quaint, taking his name from feeding on *minga*, the little black ants.

Mingaree women in the Dreaming travelled without men and set down babies in the camps, telling them not to sing or whistle—no one has ever seen the little dragon with its mate and it makes no sound. *Yugarilya* and her little sisters chased the Devilsnake Jeedarra along the shores of the Bight—he kicked up the cliffs as he ran. They chased him with their digging-sticks, but these were too small to kill him and he ran into Nullarbor caves deep under the ground. The Mingaree girls with *Yugarilya* danced and sang—

> *Wen gurardu, guradu,*
> *Ngainba ngardi,*
> *Guyer gurardi,*
> *Kangaru, kangaru, goona mulber ja!*
> *O minya!*

> *We run quickly with our sticks to kill him,*
> *But the sticks are too small.*
> *Sisters, sisters, from the same mother's womb,*
> *O small! Too small!*

The two years at Eucla, on the crest of the cliffs alone, were to Mrs Bates among the most rewarding in a vast region as yet scarcely known, the natives more primitive than any she had previously met. She tells strange tales of the desert life and death, of the dream dances of the Wanji Wanji, and of the remarkable ceremony of her own installation, among the tribal fathers, as keeper of the sacred boards with freedom of the totems, and as councillor among the tribes. The crowded pages of her hurried notes are rich in folk-lore known to nobody else on earth. In her translation, with the languages of the Stone Age, we read the stories of *Kallaia Dhoogoor Wadi*, the Emu Dreaming Men,

88

of *Burn-burn-bullaloo*, Central Australian Bellbird, of *Wanyi* and *Wiana*, men and women when the world began.

She was strangely happy among the desert people, so far now from her own ... in the long day's ending to sit at the door of her tent in the sea-breeze, sunset over the wind-curved sandhills with *Yugarilya* and the Mingaree shining, hearing the children singing, in voices soft as the wind, their song of *Nganna-marra* the Mallee-hen.... •

N-yinna gabbi gabbi bur ma lee!
Nyinna bur ma lee!
N-yinna gabbi gabbi ...

Sit down, Water, on the stones in the shade.
Sit down on the stones in the shade.
Sit down, water.

The world well lost ... she left Eucla in 1914, driving herself by camel buggy 500 miles to Adelaide, called to attend the Science Congress, seekers after knowledge, leaders of thought from all over the world. She herself delivered many lectures, going on to Melbourne and Sydney with the Congress. Refreshed in spirit, revived in ideals, scarcely was the conference over when she returned to the wilderness again, roaming here and there, Yalata, Yuria, Wandunya Water, fading out of sight in World War I.

Six

A T OOLDEA SIDING of the transcontinental railway line the Daisy Bates memorial stands where she and I first met, and where I then prophesied it one day would be.

The Lady and the Savage, *bas relief* in bronze, unpretentious but impressive, it is a world-wide classic of Australia's, strange but true.

Facing each other across ten thousand years are Kabbarli, Old Woman, regal as Queen Victoria, and Gooinmurdo of the *Meeri-kooga-da*, man-meat eaters, of the Great Victoria Desert. Kabbarli is grave and stately. Gooinmurdo, with his shield, is "noble and nude and antique". The inscription carved on the stone between them is epic though brief:

1859—1951

MRS DAISY BATES, C.B.E.

DEVOTED HER LIFE

HERE AND ELSEWHERE

TO THE WELFARE OF THE AUSTRALIAN

ABORIGINES

Swiftly and silently I greet her when I am passing by train, sealed in plate-glass and Diesel ease gliding a thousand miles a day, or glancing down on the lizard skin of Australia from a pellet of a plane flung from coast to coast, Pacific Ocean to Indian Ocean, three thousand miles in five hours of travelling at five miles high. As the jet flies, Ooldea is about midway.

It was in 1932 that I found her.

Just returned from "The Great Australian Loneliness" in the far half-circle of Western Australia—from Albany to Darwin thousands of miles in a year by air, land and sea—I planned another voyage of discovery as a pilgrim writer, following the explorers from south to north across the Centre, sailing the old Inland Sea to Carpentaria then east-about down through the Great Barrier Reef.

There were no made roads at that time in the vast hollow square of Central Australia, very few cars and trucks, no aeroplanes, no Flying Doctor. As for trains, the "Trans" continental express twice a week linked Perth with Adelaide, and so to the eastern States, Perth-Sydney and vice versa in seven days, changes at Kalgoorlie, Port Augusta, Terowie, Adelaide, Melbourne, Albury, three whole days to spare in Kalgoorlie, Adelaide, Melbourne, and delays for hours anywhere and nowhere.

To the north a South Australian train travelled twice a week to Marree. "The Ghan", Afghan express, once a fortnight chuffed and puffed from Adelaide northward a thousand miles of gibbers and sands to Alice Springs, these two new Commonwealth railways at right angles to the fanning out of the lost million square miles. Camels and donkey-teams still carried the wool away and brought supplies yearly and half-yearly to towns and stations hundreds of miles apart, changing over to packhorses and to the narrow gauge Territory railway, Birdum to Darwin, at the Top End.

The void in the map, the distant shores of mirage, were calling me with glint of gold and opal and many a Crusoe marooned. I had learnt I could travel with His Majesty's mails, gipsying to windward on some old prairie schooner from the little train towns of pub, post and police going bush once a month God Willing and, when God was unwilling, with a pack-team or camel string, in my desert odyssey to find the last of the first, the forgotten pioneers. I wanted to see their lives, to hear their stories, and to keep their memories. Above all, I wanted to see and to know my beloved country.

My first port of call was Ooldea for Mrs Daisy Bates. She was remembered in the West with some esteem and interest but rather as a female Don Quixote tilting at windmills, an odd woman out, a "character", wasting her time and money on the blacks. Very few had known her personally, none could describe her. She had been last seen at Eucla fifteen years before, all her goods and gear stacked in a camel buggy, driving across the Great Australian Bight with an Old Man of the desert and his lubra following distant smokes in South Australia. Forgotten in World War I and the financial depression that followed, she was occasionally heard of at Ooldea. An exciting corroboree of south-central desert tribes she arranged for the royal visit of Edward, Prince of Wales, in 1920—one of the highlights of his Australian tour as he passed by in the train—set her on the front page and the newsreels of the English-speaking world.

Twelve years of silence she had lived since then, but I knew she was still there. Travelling west in the Trans two years before, as we slowed down at the siding in the oven heat of a summer afternoon, "This is where Mrs Daisy

Bates is doing so much for the blacks," the conductor told me. What she could be doing was a puzzle. Natives along the Transcontinental were the poorest and most primitive, in their neglect and misery a disgrace to Australia.

Old women in reeking rags, young mothers with babies dragging at their breasts, naked children skin-and-bone with matted hair, their sad cavernous eyes a nest of flies—at the desert sidings they came begging along the trains, listless men with brummagem boomerangs for sale, silent pitiful little groups and families, knowing not a word of English. They were a novelty to travellers from overseas. Pennies and shillings pelted at them by the Trans passengers, scrapings of plates from the dining-car, fruit by regulation thrown out at the border, and offal from the butcher's shop that brought supplies for the railwaymen— these kept them alive till the next train passed by. Meagre government rations for the indigent were given out fortnightly by the police at Tarcoola and Cook, but the desert natives were mortally afraid of the police, and of other tribes. I had taken photographs of the scramble for offal, of the women and children in their rags, of an old man squatted on the ground to gnaw at the furry shin-bone of a bullock he gripped with his feet and hands. Compared with these sad travesties of the human, theirs a lifelong race in thirst and starvation over the ultimate sandhills, the natives of Kimberley and the north were Venus and Adonis in bronze.

Leaving Perth for the Central Australian journey, I had not asked Mrs Bates's permission to call lest she should warn me off or take fright and fly. I had heard she disliked publicity and was never seen from the train. I must find somewhere to stay between trains. There was no accommodation for a thousand miles across this vast south-central realm, but

G

93

Commonwealth Railways rang along the line to the ganger at Ooldea, whose wife kindly offered me a stretcher-bed on her veranda if I felt inclined. I did.

At the Karrakatta Club—of the social and intellectual élite among Perth ladies, and to which Mrs Bates had once belonged—I was given a friendly send-off at afternoon tea. They plied me with strawberries and cream-cakes.

"Better eat up!" they warned me. "Next week you'll be living on witchety grubs and carpet snake in the blacks' camp with Daisy." How little they knew of her! Later she told me she had shocked them all by inviting to lunch at the club, as her honoured guest, the scapegrace Vannie Balbuk, last old lubra of the Karrakatta people, landlords of Swan River and Perth. Balbuk, barefoot with her *booka* of mangy fur, her dilly-bag of God-knows-what, offended their sensibilities so much that some complained to the committee of the presence in the dining-room of a "disreputable old gin".

Whereupon Daisy scornfully reminded them that Balbuk, as heiress to the metropolitan area, was actually hostess to them all with the Karrakatta Club thrown in. That was in the old lady's last year of life, 1909. In the radiant city of Perth today so-called "Aboriginies" are a leaderless legion. but no truly tribal full-blood descendant of the Karrakatta Bibbulmun of Swan River has lived since then.

I set out on the Kalgoorlie express to meet the Trans, slowcoach pioneer of 1970s Indian-Pacific, with its splendour and speed, its snap-freeze luxury on greased lightning wheels slipping by at 70 to 90 m.p.h., soundless, sootless, glareless, dustless elegance and ease for overseas million-aires floating companies in nickel and steel. In 1930 the Trans was a desert marvel, the old steam train labouring for days, stopping with wallop and clang at every one of the sidings, time on the journey to make lifelong friends, concerts in the lounge through duststorms and heat-waves rising to 119 degrees.

Vacant earth and sky and lost horizons, in the wilderness was passed the "Prime Ministers", name-posts in nothing for three or four hundred miles, to the honour and glory of the Commonwealth's elder statesmen dead and alive—Forrest, Deakin, Hughes, Reid, Cook, Fisher, Watson—then plodding the Nullarbor's map of the moon by the longest railway "straight" in the world for another three hundred and thirty miles. Fifty to a hundred miles apart, the sidings were the homes of the railway men, married and single, three or four two-roomed shacks for gangers and fettlers racing on quads, breakdown gangs, scoop-gangs of camels and horses to locoes bogged in sand, or to land-slides, or to points and couplings clogged in floods and duststorms, rails endlessly buckling and slanting in inferno of heat, sleepers crumbled into wombat holes or eaten by white ants. Fettlers in perpetual motion were the coastguards in that ocean of sand for a "permanent way" here today and gone tomorrow.

On the far side of Nullarbor Plain on the third day at noon the Trans set me down at Ooldea. Passengers laughed and waved from carriage windows as it rapidly dwindled east, a sailing mirage like a ship at sea under a smoky plume, leaving me large as Gulliver on the Lilliputian shore, marooned with my suitcase, camera, typewriter, between the twin steel rails. From one of the the four little railway shacks Mrs Williams, the ganger's wife, fifteen stone of hospitality, welcomed me with outstretched hand. But why had I come to stay where all others passed by? I explained.

"Mrs Bates? Then I mustn't intrude. Let us wait till she comes. You see that white patch moving in the bush over there? She's on her way now. She spends her morning in the blacks' camp and calls here for her mail when the train is gone. . . . She speaks very softly, and never listens to camp scandal. We see very little of her, you know, and she never will let us help her in any way at all. The other day in the heat she looked so ill and worn, and it's such a long way to her camp, that I sat her down on that step and made her accept a cup of tea and a scone. I could have cried when I found a shilling under the plate after she had gone. But here she comes."

From the grey blur of mulga south of the line the white patch crossed the twin steel rails and lengthened into a rigid figure sedately pacing as a nun . . . as it drew nearer an old-fashioned fashion-plate faded and frayed with the suns of all the years. . . .

A sailor hat of straw with fly-away gossamer veil, once green now grey, over a spider-web veil tweaked under the chin; a flared dust-coat of tussore silk covering a neat white shirt-waist buttoned high to stiff polished collar and narrow pale blue ribbon tie clasped with a tarnished silver pin . . . from a trim black belt of ribbon corduroy, silver-buckled with a magnifying glass and small note-book tucked in, a trimly-tailored nine-gored skirt once black now green with age, to black stockings of fine lisle and black kid shoes, size three, high-heeled with a coquettish bow. Raggedy white gloves completed the *tout ensemble*, right hand tilting an aged black umbrella blotting us out of the view, left hand holding the mail and from its wrist dangling, *à la chatelaine* or reticule, a small-size billy-can and two or three jam-tins turned into pannikins with wire handles, all black as soot. They made a faint and rhythmic clink, step by step in the sand, with an occasional wave and jangle to chase away the flies.

Mrs Daisy Bates, I presumed.

96

As we waited in silence, with welcome smiles, the umbrella was lowered and levelled our way, as the matador fends off the bull with his cloak. But Mrs Williams settled her fifteen stone solidly in the way. "Excuse me, Mrs Bates, but this visitor is for *you*."

"Oh?"

Up flew the umbrella. I was under surveillance from under the veils, then the ragged glove lifted the green gossamer and the fish-net from a patrician little face pale in the heat, parchment fair, and a stare of polite inquiry from two very blue eyes. As a pilgrim writer interested in her work, I introduced myself. She thawed to an eagerly welcoming smile, the gloved hand with a warm clasp for mine.

"How do you do! How jolly of you to come all this way! I've read some of your writings of my beloved north-west and the mission at Beagle Bay that I helped Bishop Gibney to keep for its own rightful owners of the present day. It was nearly gone, you know, when the poor little Trappists who founded it had failed."

I regretted not asking her permission to call.

"Not at all! Why, it's fun for you to drop from the skies like this, and we'll have so much to say. Are you staying with this fettler's wife?" A wave of the hand to the *hoi polloi*. I thanked Mrs Williams for her kind hospitality, but Daisy had other ideas.

"Will you walk with me to my camp about a mile away? It's as poor as wood, but if you would dare to share my very primitive life, it would be such a delight to me."

So I asked Mrs Williams would she mind if I changed my mind. She indulgently smiled.

"Don't change your mind till you see!" Daisy warned. "Leave the luggage here and come over for a cup of tea. If it's too crude and rough, I'll understand. Mrs Williams, if we're not back by the time the sun's *that way*"—she waved blackfellow fashion to two hours down the sky—"you will please send one of the children for Gooinmurdoo to come with my wheelbarrow and bring this luggage to my camp."

Mrs Williams had taken no umbrage. Reduced to the role of gamekeeper's wife when Milady is driving around, she noted instructions very respectfully. Umbrella slanted against the fiery sun, we wended our way sedately pacing to the tintinnabulation of the tins and the buzzing of the flies. Arm in arm, we were friends.

Her little ladyship—for so, indeed, she seemed—from weariness of labour in the heat, suddenly meeting a kindred soul, was electrified in interest and in energy.

"Forgive me, my dear, if I appeared to pass you by. I thought you were somebody's niece. Nobody ever leaves the train in a thousand miles except the gangers' and fettlers' families. They all live for the trains with the exception of me. Very good people in their way—we're pleasant neighbours but never friends. It wouldn't do in my work for the natives, who look on me as one of themselves. I belong to them. I'm *Dhoogoor Dhuga*, an old Spirit-Woman of the Dreaming, don't you know? Their grandmother *Kabbarli*. If I hobnobbed with the white people I'd lose my tribal significance, and then again, I must not hunt with the hare and the hounds. I have strongly objected to some of the white people's tricks and meannesses to them. They set them to work with no pay but the scrapings of the plates . . . or they send them to beg on the trains and sell them a crust of bread for a two-shilling piece, or a billy of old stale tea and a pound of flour for a ten-shilling note—ugly and underhand things that white people everywhere do to this poor inarticulate race that never retaliates, never even sees their trickery. That's what I try to repay!"

From the crest of a sandhill she waved to the haze of horizons north-west—not a fence, not a roof, not a sign of civilization then between this skeleton railway and the Indian Ocean two thousand miles away. Tawny-dark sandhills rippled with wind ribbed away to the north, a thousand miles of uninhabited country to the Musgrave and Hann ranges and another thousand to Victoria River in the Northern Territory. Waving with closed hand, in the Aboriginal gesture, never pointing, bad magic, she told me of Mount Daisy Bates on the Western Australian border, known to her natives and named for her by Frank Hann, the lone, lame explorer. Right about turn and the ragged glove gestured south.

"There's nothing down there to the shores of the Southern Ocean but one or two stations you'd never find," she said. "I travelled across in a camel buggy seventeen years ago from Williambi Water at Eyre's Patch to Wandunya Water near Fowler's Bay by no road at all, and as yet it hasn't changed. Eastward are the big salt lakes, westward the Nullarbor Plain. No trees. This is the last of the mulga for 450 miles by 330 miles of nothing whatever but scorched earth and black cinders of saltbush that are floods five feet deep and a fairy veil of wildflowers when it rains—and it rains once in seven years." We smiled.

She dramatized her speech and waited for the smiles. So excited she was with a listener in the hours, years, of silence, that present and past were scrambled with geographies, histories, scenes, Aboriginal legends, sharing thoughts that crowded a remarkably receptive and perceptive mind, keenly observant always of people, places and things.

Quite often she was lost for a word, substituting an Aboriginal word, or, playfully, "*Gigglywinks!* What am I trying to say? So long I've been speaking only to the natives in so many of their languages that mine's gone rusty. They have a much broader larynx than ours for a much wider range of sounds, some more musical—bird-calls for instance—some that coarsen the mouth. If I croak at you, pray forgive me. They have a proverb, don't you know, the South-central tribes. *Maamu waibela wonga*—literally, debil white-man speech—the Devil speaks English." We smiled. There was certainly nothing lost of her fluency and her wit.

We talked of mysterious Nullarbor, the cracked old roof of catacombs of dead limestone caverns with lakes of never a ripple down there in the black dark, of tunnels where the sea-winds roar and roll with a rumble of drums ninety miles from the sea, or whistle and howl to blowholes rising and falling with ebb and flow of tides in the Great Australian Bight, the noise of the trains reverberant for miles. The blacks were terrified of the Plain—*Oondiri*, thunder—a no-man's-land of death by hunger and thirst. They were horrified when *Ganba* came to life in the first crossing of the Transcontinental, a dragon screeching and puffing smoke, baleful eyes in the night. Some of them died of fright.

Nearly all the tribal groups of the south were gone. Daisy had come to defend them, she said, when the construction gangs of a thousand men in a thousand miles, five years building the line, whipped them away from their waters and hunting-grounds, or corrupted them with drink and disease, taking their women as prostitutes, brawling and fighting. In the aftermath of World War I, in the plague of pneumonic influenza, in the turbulence of industrial troubles, strikes, settlement of returned soldiers and provision for wives and children of those never to return, out of sight, out of mind, were the Aboriginal Australians. With no hope of government assistance, it was then she sold her share in the station property to provide the daily bread of the waifs and strays and her own. She invariably praised her Adelaide bankers for their helpfulness over many years in shepherding her resources while there were any at all.

She was one of the first women to live on the Transcontinental. "The biggest railway camps," she said, "and the biggest native camps were here at Ooldea Soak, the main water supply of the line. That was why I came."

Ooldea Water—*Yooldil-gabbi* its Aboriginal name—was a miracle storage of many thousands of gallons of pure filtered water in a hollow of the sandhills veiled by the sand. In half a million square miles of arid land with only a few surface waters, in the worst droughts it never failed as the hope and salvation for centuries and generations of the desert tribes. Nomad groups of men, women and children, walking for water and food all their lives, would travel down by the rock-holes, springs and wells that soon dried, sometimes a race with death to Yooldil, to camp for many moons waiting for rain in a muster there of affiliated tribes. Kangaroo and emu, wombats, boodie rats, birds, lizards, sharing the waters, provided them with game. A siege of man against nature in the Stone Age, it was sanctuary to all, stage of the great corroborees, man-makings, peace-makings, a depot for trade and the end of the great trade route in barter of red and yellow ochres, rainstones, pliable wood for boomerangs and spears, *pituri* the bush tobacco, medicine berries, furstring, *mindree* gum, pearl-shell years on the way from Broome and Darwin, products of various zones and regions in between and all shapes and sizes of stones from quartz to haematite and diorite, for axe-heads, spearheads, weapons, utensils, tools, circumcision knives, murder knives. They whittled away the days, singing away the nights till the rains, when after the farewell orgies, wife-stealings, revenges, they made for home again. So it went on from the days of the

Dreaming, their legends and letter-stick maps bringing them down in the drought years, until the white man came with his monster train.

Ooldea Waters, the only plentiful supplies in what he called a "waterless waste", were the one great natural resource in the building of the line. Pumped and piped to the siding for the locomotives and the labour camps at the rate of 70,000 gallons a day for five years or more, they were dwindling away.

"I set my camp by the pipeline in 1917," Mrs Bates told me, "just turning a tap into cool fresh waters flowing by. Some said they were artesian, to give a million gallons a day. Some said underground rivers, or perpetual springs. Engineers and surveyors were sent to bore and dam and harness, to read the riddle and so to increase the flow. But, alas, when they pierced the blue clay foundations twenty or thirty feet down the waters were lost for ever, seeping through the sands. It was a very remarkable and extensive sub-artesian storage. Now it's only a hollow in the sandhills, dry as a bone. We have to ration between us the water brought by the trains from Port Augusta and Karonie, east and west, to fill tanks at the sidings all the way along. I carry mine in kerosene tins for a mile and more.

"But the poor perishing wanderers of south-central deserts still come to find it over the burning sands, for there's no way of their knowing that Yooldil-gabbi is for ever gone. Its own people are dead. I helped to bury eleven of them about me here in the sandhills. My natives now are those creatures of the desert, of pitiful savagery in their chronic hunger. As Meeri-kooga-da, the Man-meat Eaters, they are known to neighbouring tribes. In those stark ribs of the sandhills where nothing lives, nothing can be wasted. A man may eat parts of a man when he dies, flesh, for strength and survival. It is half ritual, half appetite. A woman may eat her new-born baby.

"There's a woman here now with that loathsome craving. Minmilla. Her last child was eaten at birth. She is about to give birth to another, and she is gone from the camp. Neither her man nor I can track her. Her little son is with her, Thannana, a child of five. He shared the last one with her! I've promised them *balya mai*, that is, good tucker, flour, tea and sugar for a moon, if they bring the baby in alive."

At this stage I interrupted Mrs Bates's fluent monologue, asking for proof of her statement.

Throughout Western Australia and the Northern Territory, and in all other States, in my careful research I had found no official record of cannibal customs, habits of propensities, and not one instance where evidence of the crime had been tendered as exhibit in an Australian court of law. So far as I knew, it was never proved by Exhibit A of the bones or remains. Some of the old bushmen told such tales, rumours, seldom of their own knowledge, and the accusation was made in tall stories, namely in de Rougemont's Adventures, and in Richard Dehen's *The Sower of the Wind*, a novel wherein a beautiful half-caste girl from Broome, educated in Paris, comes back to the north-west, marries, and polishes off her child. The natives themselves have often admitted the guilt of the race, but blaming always an enemy tribe. When eager to please, they may even confess it, but long ago and far away with details vague. These doubts I clearly expressed to Mrs Bates.

She was convinced, and very emphatic. "My dear child, I have seen the grisly remains of a newborn baby cooked and eaten here at Ooldea by its mother, a woman named Ngan-ngauera, and you will find the evidence you demand of me in the Adelaide Museum. All the Aboriginal tribes of my long experience among them, with the exception of the Bibbulmun of the south-west, racially distinct from the later migration—men, women and children made no secret to me of the fact that they were cannibally inclined. Will you come with me to find Minmilla, and track down the evidence I cartainly hope we don't find?"

I agreed, and the subject was changed. "I earnestly trust," I said, "that you're keeping your own historical records of the tribes you have known, a knowledge unique and a treasure to Australia."

She replied, "But that's my reason for being! Thirty years of my gathering—laws, beliefs, customs, languages, legends, tools, weapons, corroborees, poison bones—all the giggly-winks they carry about, the corroborees, the ceremonies, the devils that haunt them, the songs they sing! You'll see my anthropologies at my camp, thousands of notes higgledy-piggledy, written on anything, envelopes, bills, margins of books, what I could find where they never heard of writing paper and ink! Nobody else could know what I mean, but I live for the day, and they're all according to the book, scientifically speaking. I travelled with the Cambridge Research Expedition in Western Australia in 1914 as guide and interpreter, adviser and so on—an invaluable insight for me into the form. They wanted me to come home to Cambridge and take a degree, but my poor friendless natives in their last years in a lost world and my field work in a million square miles in my own way were more to me than any university."

In reminiscence, again she smiled. "They ran out of funds, and never could have completed their work had it not been for me. I approached a wealthy pastoralist, Sam Mackay of Mundabullangana Station near Port Hedland.

Quite impudently I told him he owed his fortune to Western Australia and to its native people, especially for their land and their labour, and asked him to contribute to funds of the expedition for knowledge and research in the interests of posterity. Will you believe it? He wrote a cheque for £2,000 and handed it to me. He was a great lady's man but he wasn't a man I could kiss. I danced in glee!"

Skyward sailed the umbrella. A merry and mischievous coquette wheeled in the sand and laughed at me. Then she continued seriously, "So the good work went on, one of our first expeditions from a university. Several books were written by its members, including a novel *Where Bonds Are Loosed*, by Grant Watson. The leader became an Oxford professor of anthropology. They were with me at Dorre and Bernier islands. Remind me to tell you of the cruelty, the horror and the heartbreak to the poor old natives on those desolate isles in the sea. . . . But here we come to my camp, just over the rise."

In remembering Kabbarli, as in the writing of her book, *The Passing of the Aborigines*, I do not quote her verbatim exactly but from my notes at that time, which I still keep for reference, and they are transposed by me. She never made any corrections or contradictions in her material in the typewritten manuscript as presented by me, true to the trend and sequence of events, to her character, sentiments, her manner of speaking.

"Her voice was ever soft, gentle and low." In all the years I knew her I was never to hear it raised, but it was never monotonous . . . on the contrary. The deep tones, rounded vowels, the light and shade, quick-change from tragedy to gaiety and back again to grief, from our first meeting were echoing in my mind, reminding me of some poetic prose.

I had it, J. M. Synge! *The Tinker's Wedding. Riders to the Sea.*

She was Irish, it suddenly dawned on me. That explained everything, the idealism, endurance, self-sacrifice, the prejudice and pride, her fearlessness "agin the government" and her wilfulness "nohow contrariwise", all her intuitions and inhibitions, her delight in folk-lore, her perpetual adoration of royalty, and at the same time the life-long loyalty to the lost cause of a lost people with all their sins and sorrows in her always loving heart and mind.

Seven

I F WALDEN POND is a shrine of Thoreau's immortality, a
dip in the sands of Ooldea a mile north of the siding
keeps Daisy's memory. There she lived alone through
seventeen years of long and silent days and nights.

A four-square brush fence of withered mulga branches
enclosed an acre or two of stunted scrub, the gateway a pile
of prickle-bush, "dead finish", to hold trespassers at bay. In
the middle was a tent, ten feet by eight, with buckets, tin
dishes and various cans slanted in the guy-ropes round it, a
forlorn hope to catch a sudden rain from those blinding blue
skies.

Twenty feet in front of the tent was a circle of white ash,
above it a gypsy trident with a billy-can on a hook. A
blackened jam-tin half full of rice and two potatoes roasting
in their wrinkled skins were in the smouldering coals.

A 500-gallon tank rusted into holes, turned over on its
side, was her library, with sapling shelves for about a hundred well-worn tomes. On a little rise a crude bush ladder
of five rungs climbed to a rickety bough shade, its bandy
props leaning against the brush fence.

"My observatory . . . for aboriginal astronomies," she explained. "They tell me their legends and draw their constellations in the sand and I look them out by comparing them with ours."

Bathroom was a shower from a perforated potato tin hanging in a tree and a cubby-house convenience with a long shaft, a bottle of phenyle, a tin of sand, and a high brush fence all round. A few feet from the front door, if so the prickle-bush could be called, Ooldea pipe-line was a hollow mockery, bone-dry for years but the natives' waiting-room outside the breakwind, where they patiently awaited her attention and where rations were given out.

"I have my meal in the twilight when they've all gone home," she said. "They won't travel a yard at night for fear of devils in the dark. The day is theirs but the night is mine." She prodded out the potatoes with a long wire toasting-fork. "I'm not a vegetarian, oh no. I get a little meat from the Tea-and-Sugar train, but it goes bad in a few hours in the heat, and the flies are murder. The tinned butter is smelly yellow oil. So I don't bother with those things much. I have eggs and cheese and jam—I drink lashings of tea with toast and jam, and that powdered milk is very nourishing."

She filled the billy from a waterbag hanging in a tree and set it on the coals, then made a tragicomic little face under the veil.

"I must confess to you I can't cook. I've never learnt to cook. Isn't that disgraceful of me? But I have two saucepans and a frying-pan, and a camp bed with sheets and towels, and another tent that I'll rig for you if you'll stay. Do stay!"

Nothing could make me happier. Far in the north-west and the Territory I had met Women of the Loneliness who watched the road for years, praying for a woman to come to stay. They never stopped talking in the first couple of days. We sat on canvas stools with two pretty little cups and saucers—English china, no pannikins, please, for afternoon tea. Then we rigged another ten-by-eight between two mulga-trees and made the stretcher bed, a flimsy camp but quite enough for me.

"I always keep these ready in case a friend should come," she said, "a woman-friend, that is. I daren't invite a gentleman to set a foot inside that breakwind, or even be seen talking to him alone, or my reputation's gone as Kabbarli. There's only one association of a woman and a man together that the natives understand, and that soft impeachment must never apply to me. I'm more a spirit, you know. It can be quite embarrassing. I had to refuse admission one day to a bishop who came a-visiting me. An anthropologist from Sydney University knocked on the ridge-pole of my tent when the natives were about. I ordered him out but he didn't want to go, so I burrowed through the breakwind and fled him from tree to tree. I'm quite sure he went back and reported my insanity."

She pinned up the flap of the tent with a gracious, "Make yourself at home, my dear. This is my little world for sleeping and waking, reading and writing, everything that's me. See my pictures on the wall!" Laughing, she waved to the shadow-branches of mulga on the white translucency of the canvas, a Japanese spray *bonsai* changing every hour in sun or moonlight. "That's one of the chiefest joys of living in a tent," she said, "with the birds, the lizards and small furry friends that come to call on me."

Her stretcher bed was neat with 'roo-skin rug and bush net, the linen Isabelline from poor water but spotlessly clean. On the sand floor a goat-skin mat was spread. An iron stand with an enamel dish held soap and towel, hung on a nail above it a hand-mirror four-by-four, inches not feet, re-

H

flecting the face, no more—no time for vanity. The table in the corner was four-by-four feet, half of it cleared for dining, crockery in a stack, cutlery two of each, tea-set and salt and pepper twins. The other half was a leaning tower of Manila folders of rough manuscript, litter of letters, pens, ink, a portable typewriter seldom used and then by the hunt-and-peck system with two fingers—she called it a "gigglywinks". Lighting installations were a hurricane lamp on a post and two candles in candlesticks. Underneath was a large tin trunk and beside it two more, one on the other, with a tablecloth and a two-decker tin safe. These were her wardrobe and store. Two folding chairs completed the list, and a deck-chair for hot nights, just outside the door.

One day she opened the trunks and showed me the harvest of the years. The large trunk was crammed with manuscript, the thirty-three years of notes and jottings on Aboriginal lore she had written by sun or moon or firelight, unique, obscure and infinitely precious knowledge by the hundredweight scribbled in old diary books, dog-eared pads, the backs of envelopes, multi-million pages torn and yellow with age, rusty and dusty with years of outback trails, some in the languages of tribes extinct known only to her. From these her life's story would later be compiled, the strangest memoirs, life and letters, ever written by a woman. In time, I would know them well.

The second trunk held the Quality Street suits, coats, toques, shoes, safe from moth and rust in unbleached linen bags with camphor balls. Of architecture rather than tailoring, and of finest materials, they belonged to the age when mothers of families in last wills and testaments bequeathed to their daughters their best and second-best dresses complete with bugles, beads and jewelleries. She assured me her dressing was no "image" of affectation but common sense and economy. What nonsense to yearn for hobble skirts, split skirts and horrors of the vogue on the Madman's Track to the Ophthalmia Range! So far from cities, why chop and change with so much needed to feed the natives?

But the famous gloves, cheap cotton gloves by the dozen, were no absurdity, a first necessity in the native camps of dirt and lice, venereal disease and leprosy. "Where rubber gloves would perish in the heat, these can be boiled in Lysol," she said, "or buried with the dead when I bury the dead."

There, too, was her evening-dress, tissued in its folds, sacheted with mignonette, fichu, flounces, train sculptured in taffetas once white now ivory, with silken mittens and satin shoes so small that Cinderella might have lost one at the ball. From a heart-shaped velvet case came an exquisite miniature four hundred years old, painted in France, of a great-great—grandmother, don't you know?—her family heirloom, and her only jewellery not sold. I regret I forget the artist's name.

A bundle of treasured photographs was packed with the underclothes—four-decker petticoats, twenty-five button camisoles, commodious night-gowns neck to toes, chemises, combinations, drawers, frills below the knees, all to be lashed down with hooks and eyes, baby-ribbon threaded through lace at elbows and knees and tied with bows. Some neatly darned, all were thinning into fringes and holes. Underneath was her household linen—"My napery, don't you know? It's good in parts, like the curate's egg.

"I made friends with a needle as a very small child at grandma's knee," she told me. "I can do the most minute embroideries, but I can't use a machine, and I couldn't make myself a pair of drawers to save my life. We weren't supposed to know such things."

Under the underclothes she kept the clothing for the natives, first steps in civilization, the rough "blackfella" trousers and shirts, bright cheap print dresses for women and girls, cattlemen's gaudy handkerchiefs, coarse towels, turkey red and striped blue galatea by the yard.

"Nothing good. They trade it or wear it to a dirty rag in a day. It grieves me to see them in this ugly rubbish, but I refuse to give them cast-offs of the white people, passed round among them and spreading disease. They're much better in their skins dry-cleaned by the sun and wind, but they must be clothed for their contacts here and in the towns. The police at Tarcoola give them a blanket and billy-can, with a bit of flour, tea and sugar once a fortnight, but they're afraid to go near the police. Tarcoola's three hundred miles on among strange blacks feared by these poor desert waifs. They come in from a journey of maybe a thousand miles, foot-walking naked on their bare burnt feet and nearly dead of hunger and thirst. They're looking for Yooldil-gabbi at journey's end since the Dreaming—and Yooldil-gabbi's gone. They've heard that Kabbarli is a friend. I see their queer head-dresses and shadowy shapes above the breakwind in the early morning, and in twos and threes they'll sit by the pipe-line till I take heed of them—that's the Aboriginal way of approaching a stranger's camp in peace. They know no English, but I speak the desert language. It's one great homogeneous language from here to Gregory's Salt Sea. Just how benighted and primitive they are you'll see by what I have here."

She opened the third trunk, her chamber of horrors. Death-bones! Seven or eight of the gruesome things from two to four inches long. It is always a human bone to kill, from the arm, or leg, or collar-bone of a murdered man, sharpened to a vicious point or flat and serrated to leaf-shape with a claw at the end. Each one is strung on a dead man's hair and wrapped in bloody emu-feathers. Some were spiralled with eaglehawk down stuck on with blood and gum, some banded and scratched with minute design of dots or wavy lines to number the victims, sealed with a lump of gum to hold in the poison when not in use. Pointing the bone is not a tribal rite but devilry of a witch-man, often a hired assassin. A notorious bone can be hired or borrowed for the job. When a vendetta is in the air, the wizard wears it on a hair-string a-dangle at the back of his neck, terrifying the camp like a man with a gun. Soon the victim knows it is for him—a fatal hypnotic power, melancholia, hysteria, coma, death. It kills quickly or slowly, no escape, murder by malice, the eerie power of evil thought.

Ulalya darrga at Eucla, *wilyuru*, Oodnadatta, *wuruguru*, Cooper's Creek, it has many names. One of the best, and worst, from Glen Ferdinand in the Rawlinson Range, Mrs Bates had presented to the Prince of Wales—"Three inches long," she told me, "a beautiful deep ivory bevelled flat and barbed, a work of art centuries old in evil hate, the ends needle-sharp, one dipped in blood, for blood-poisoning, the other charred to inject a burning fire into liver, lungs and heart. Circles and dots, the Old Man said, had once destroyed a whole tribe."

From brown paper parcels she unrolled the blackest of magics, *mirri mobburn* of Eucla, dead men's spirit bones twined with their hair and hooked to catch souls; kangaroo and emu bones for the lesser poisons; bad medicine stones to choke and fester; mulga and corkwood whittled into snake-shapes and crude animal forms; poison sticks; bird-claws in a ball of *mindree* gum. *Guriyarra* was a double bone to kill man and wife together in one fell shot, or more likely man and the murderer's wife.

The white quartz knives of *kurdaitcha* were there, daggers with haft of clay and sheath of bark, and four pairs of *kurdaitcha* shoes—

Jinnabooka! Feather-foot! Trackless terror of the spinifex, ritual murder-cult of paleolithic man—*kurdaitcha* is tribal, a secret society of four or five controlled by councils of the Old Men. They travel to kill. When sentence of death is passed on their own runaways or a raid planned on a neighbouring camp, they are the firing squad, the Commandos, the executioners. Mission invisible! They stripe their bodies with white to be optical illusions, paint their faces with demon-designs masked and hooded, much the same as the Ku-Klux Klan. They make for themselves and wear crude moccasins of emu feathers strung on fur-string and stitched with sinews, cemented together with blood and gum, haircord fastenings round the ankles.

When the word is given they set out, skulls and ribs, spectres, to travel the two twilights, sometimes many days and miles, before they strike. Half-human, half-supernatural devil, they mesmerize the tribes through which they pass. Nobody dares to see them and give warning. Running over the stones, leaping from bush to bush, even on the sand their flimsy slippers of death leave no track of a man. They "daylight" a sleeping camp, spearing, stabbing, strangling, vanishing like shadows, unrecognized, unheard and unseen, a terror of the dawn. When *kurdaitcha* men are about the tribes of innocent bystanders are paralysed with fear. I have heard of them only in Central Australia and south. Daisy called them *jinna arbil*, Ooldea language, hidden feet.

Full of such devilries was the Third Trunk at Kabbarli's tent door,

> *Wi' mair o' horrible an' awfu'*
> *That e'en to name would be unlawfu'* . . .

114

the smell of evil, curses and spells in bones, stone and images of hate in the sorcerer's blackest arts. Whenever a new "mob", as she called them, arrived, her first thought was to take possession of murder gear that scared the others out of their wits all along the line.

She was not a collector of Aboriginal curios. Their sacred tribal objects—*churinga, wanningi,* totem boards, initiation knives, rain and fertility stones, phallic symbols and man-making regalia, ceremonial spears, stone tools, letter-sticks, music-sticks, utensils and charms, in her time authentic and of unique interest, she never claimed. In their councils and corroborees she never interfered.

"Blackfella business", forbidden by the missionaries as heathen and idolatrous, she recognized as the oldest religion in the world and of its first social systems and administrations, benignant rather than malignant, comparable with our own in its comprehensions, in its interpretations as just and unjust, as wise and unwise. Their human nature in antiquity, she felt, was never realized in the new Australia, their laws and customs—apart from a few savageries—to be respected as the other fellow's mind and a most valuable insight into the childhood of *homo sapiens.* In the Old Stone Age, also, murder was a mystery and a capital crime, so that the Third Trunk was more of a police museum with its reek of death in madness and in fear. Incidentally, it kept Kabbarli safe from any intrusion, any "Cheeky" attack, with all those devils assorted to let loose on them.

Not that she depended solely on supernatural protection or the saintly armour of Women of the Dreaming in that lonely place. By the neon-red coals in bone-white ash of the mulga, as we sat late into the night over cups of tea, remembering the nightly arc of Western Australia we had both travelled for knowledge of its people, white and Aboriginal, came the

eldritch wailing of a pack of dingoes in the sandhills near
. . . nearer, shrill and eerie as the howls of sinners in hell.

"I'll soon fix those gentlemen!" said she, and quick as a
wink was into the tent and out of it with a six-chambered
revolver, .32 pointing bone of the twentieth century, that
she fired into the trees with a packet-of-crackers racket receding into the silence with "Gelert's dying yell"—no harm
done even to the wild dogs.

"I keep this," she told me, "not for my natives, heaven
forbid, but for the wild white men passing by in these
depression years. Hundreds are jumping the rattler, don't
you know, out of the cities on the dole and out of the jails
walking round Australia. The poor benighted savages I can
trust, but not these. I doubt I could fire it at a man, but how
would he know?"

Always in the bush she was up and dressed at four in the
morning, still in the starlight, making tea, warbling back to
the magpies, echoing the oboe notes of *Burn-burn-boolooloo*,
Central Australian crested bell-bird. By their native names
she greeted her daily visitors among the small wild creatures,
furry marsupial friends, stumpy goanna and frilled lizard,
little bicycle lizard pedalling round and *Moloch horridus*,
miniature medieval dragon knobbed and scaled, his angry
gape and fiery hues belying his gentle nature and the white
man's name of "mountain devil" wide of the mark as he
lives on the hot sandy plains. In natural history Daisy had
a child's delight, even in this barren place. Her birdbooks
and manuscripts were full of straggly notes and of legends
and totem tales of the small fry of the sandhills and she
longed to complete a new southern hemisphere zodiac and
mythologies from all-Australian fauna and flora.

Our breakfast was tea and toast again, then she prepared
for the natives the tins of boiled rice, sago, macaroni or other

116

"hobble-gobble" as she called it, with beef extract or powdered milk for proteins. The precious water for washing up, used four or five times, that I hastily threw away because four or five dead flies were there floating, brought me a curt reminder that every drop must be carried a laborious mile in sunstroke heat or brought by native labour that cost her a shilling a time. Flies, though revolting, must be dredged off, water used and used till only a sprinkle was left and that to lay the dust. Laundry was a tin dish and one flat-iron on the coals, her collars and cuffs posted to Port Augusta, a thousand miles there and back once a month. The daily bath was a once-over with a washer and a perforated jam-tin shower to sluice away the soap from above.

Sun-time was our clock. By noon we must be at the blacks' camp, two miles across the line. Screeches and squalls of their dogs—thirty or forty cringing curs, ribs, whip-tails and yellow eyes, a cross between lizard and hound—were silenced with curses as Kabbarli came in sight. She never could keep a dog or cat as friend because "white-fella dogs" fight "blackfella dogs" to the death and chase and terrify the blacks, a racial prejudice as marked as that of their masters. Cats killed all the rare little marsupials and birds.

Her first call in the native camp was a little Gagool of a crippled woman sixty years old, the size of a starving child of ten, Jinnawillee, Angry Foot, then two of the Old Men, one rheumatic, one rheumy and blind. Knowing the tribal law that all food must be shared, she fed them by hand, and roundly scolded Jinnawillee for hiding a crust in her closed fist to give to a grown-up son—as women must do, providing all but meat for the men.

Young men with their hair in chignons, the middle-aged with mud curls, Moses and Aaron with long flowing hair, came to her with their problems—flighty wives, defiant daughters and sons, bullying bosses, enemies "singing" them. She called them by their Aboriginal names according to their place in the tribes—to the white man's knack of treating them as "boys" with contemptuous nicknames such as Spider and Jack the Ripper she objected. Gravely and courteously she listened to their troubles, advising, forbidding or reproaching them, or promising to write helpful letters to authorities. In straightforward English and their own languages she discussed their sicknesses, afflictions: the simpler medical needs for her own treatment, and in accidents or serious ills she made immediate contact with hospital doctors at Port Augusta, arranging their railway passages and notifying the police. She was never a prude in explaining their sexual habits and anatomies—penis, scrotum, testicles, vulvotomy and the venereal diseases—though I am quite sure she would be appalled at the present smart theatrical cult of "ugly" four-letter words, unpronounceable, unthinkable, perhaps unknown to a lady of her day and age.

She had no special medical knowledge or training as a nurse. She used "Grandmother's remedies", with cleanliness and common sense, *Materia Medica* and *Family Doctor* her guide-books in the bush for treatments, and a medicine chest of much in little for their common ills. Condy's Crystals, Friar's Balsam, eucalyptus, Carron oil for burns, cod liver oil, senna tea, boracic to bathe bung eyes, ointments, liniments and bandages, insectibanes for lice with disinfectants —such as these were her stock-in-trade, as physician-in-ordinary to all camps, with a bedside manner of cheerfulness, of gentle sympathy and jokes, that worked wonders. She was among them night and day in epidemics of measles, influenza, fevers. They died in her camps not of neglect but

118

usually of age, and when they were dying she sat with them for hours, to keep away the devils of death and fear by her own faith and theirs in a loving Father and a haven of rest and peace beyond the grave . . . her life's pilgrimage of graves by the orphan waters of Australia.

Eight

FOR SO LONG the friend and familiar of death in the camps, the only white mourner at the wailings and gnashings of weird tree-burials all the years, at Ooldea she seemed to be a Woman of the Sorrows, a traveller from Eternity with her memories and mythologies. Never again, among her own people in cities, would she leave me with such a strange impression of one superhumanly spiritual, not old but ageless . . . as some of the natives believed her, a Sun-fire woman, a salamander.

Self-centred in her thoughts, utterly selfless in her needs, she seemed as one living on light and air. This was not far from the truth. There was a time, she told me, when she had only porridge to share. Her last little property in real estate, a pleasant home for her old age on the hill at South Perth, had gone the way of the station in the Ophthalmia Range and all else that was hers. I think she was now sharing with the natives a pension of a couple of pounds a week, but she never mentioned money. Sympathy or patronage would have been odious to her. I never heard her express a regret or a word of self-pity in the loneliness. She mentioned her son and her grandchildren affectionately. I have often wondered if her perpetual adoration of the royal family, her identification with the aristocrat, and in the balance her life's devotion to the abjectly pitiful and oppressed, were filling the vacuum in a loving heart with dream people, the world's most favoured and the world's least.

She sincerely loved the Aborigines and never failed them. There was no false glorification. She was not blind to their failings and their savageries. On the contrary, she accused them unjustly at times, but in forgiveness of a primitive race. Many were her true friends regardless of colour and class. For their gentleness, or endurance, or nobility, or for their merry natures as rapscallions, she remembered them to the end. Beside a deserted wurley or when she was speaking of the dead, her voice became an elegy . . . "*Koordal winjaka*, their hearts have ceased to beat."

With her digging-stick, *wanna*, emblem of a woman, she slipped back into her Aboriginal mind. Hers alone was the poetry of the Dreaming, a literature of languages, classics and legends unknown to the rest of the world. As each day we trudged for miles, searching for Minmilla, we rambled in pre-history of the most ancient times, in the Origin of Species when the totemic ancestry of Terra Australia—element, animal, bird, lizard, plant—were the life-givers and the law-givers in the land, man's first concept of how things came to be, and his conscious kinship in evolution with all creation. In those young days the nature spirits were much closer, much closer the memory of the ages when giants walked the earth. Kabbarli conjured them back again at Ooldea.

To the eastward *Maalu*, Spirit Kangaroo, sent his play boomerang whirling round and round to make the great salt lakes where skulls and skeletons of *Wardanunga*, wombat-diprotodon, and *Kadimookera*, saurian, lay centuries deep in the sand dunes and the last brine pools of the old inland sea. To the westward when Nullarbor Plain was a garden, Jeedarra, the fiery serpent, scorched it to cinders with the flame of his breath, devoured all the *beru* and *maia*, the game and vegetation, leaving ashes of earth in a hell of thirst, *Oondiri,* bald, as he gulped down its waters and coiled in the dry caves beneath to haunt and destroy. But other tribes said that the Plain was the big burnt circle where *Beera* the Moon sat down when, hunting there with his dogs, he had a fight with *Ginnega*, Native Cat. Away to the northward the gibber plains were made by *Jurr Jurr* the Night Owl, who smashed to atoms the stony hills to please his wife, *Mulgaru*, Boodie Rat. He had stolen her from her country and she was afraid in the ranges, having always lived on the sandy flat. *Wilba* the Wallaby kicked up the sandhills around Ooldea Soak over the skin bag of precious waters hidden there by *Karrbijji*, Marsupial Mouse, when he was chased by *Ngabbula*, Spike-backed lizard, speared by *Kallaia*, Emu—you can see the spears in Ngabbula's back.

All these were once among the totem folk around Ooldea Soak,—"*Yooldil-gabbi*, water sit down"—each group in its own valley and coming from afar in times of drought. They brought payment for the water they used, and items of trade from their own countries, pituri tobacco, rainstones, red and yellow ochres, stone for the blades and scrapers of knives and tools, fibre-string and birds' feathers, wood for the making of boomerangs and spears, for music-sticks and letter-sticks, pearl-shell years on the way from the Indian Ocean coast. Treasures of a multitude down through the centuries may still be found in the sands around Ooldea Soak.

The living men and women we met, *nunga* and *wiani*, might be a Banded Goanna from Wandunya water and a

Wild Cherry from Boundary Dam, who had eloped together
—a scandal of the Stone Age. Their marriage was wrong
and had set the spears and kylees flying in a fight when the
rightful husband tracked them up, a Feather-tailed Rat. In
those barren sands the men were still hunting their food as
it ran—though now mostly rabbits. The women, *wiani*,
could fill their *dhaggula*, wooden scoops, with quandong,
the native peach, mulga apples, yam roots, wild cucumber,
grass seeds, *wonganu*, pounded to flour between two stones,
birds' eggs and lizards' eggs or the birds and lizards themselves, so many life-sustainers in the grey of the bush unseen
by civilized man. Kabbarli knew them and could tell
strangers where they might be found. She drew the line
at Aboriginal diet. I never heard of her tackling stumpy
goanna, witchety grub or white ants.

In the starry nights we climbed the rickety ladder to the
withered branch of a bench she called her observatory, to
travel the Road of the Dreaming, *Dhoogoor Yuara*, where
all the stars were mustering in to the heavenly waterholes
and the Milky Way, the River that Never Dries. At Ooldea
she added and completed many major legends from south-
central deserts, sitting aloft for a patient hour or two with
a few of the Old People sprawled below outside the breakwind. They drew maps with a stick in the sand of Aboriginal
constellations, the totemic zodiacal signs, the fixed stars and
pilgrim planets—grand march of the skies at night with all
tribes on the move in the glittering dust of nebulae following
their cult heroes akin to the Greek gods . . . *Kata*, Heads. . . .

Jupiter and Venus, morning and evening star, were Maalu
and Kulbir, red and grey Kangaroos, a night between them
on the same path. The black void in the Milky Way is
Kallaia, Emu, his head in the Coal Sack, as we say, his long

neck, wings, legs, in the dark lanes of the Greek zodiac, between Aquila and Lyra his nebulous tail. Through all their lives the Emu totem men must never look at him:

Kallaia dhoogoor waddi
Ngai-u-ongu eelung.

Emu Dreaming Man,
I look! I die!

Southern Cross is *Walja-jinna*, the Eaglehawk's Track, with *Dhurding*, the Pointers, his Club, near by. Never point at Magellan's Clouds, *Murgaru*, *O-imbu*, the Right-handed and Left-handed Brothers who snatch away the dead. *Kogolongo* is Mars, Black Cockatoo with red feather in his tail. Altair is *Kangga Ngoonju*, Crow Mother, with Delphinus, her Crow boys,—Vega in Lyra is *Gibbera*, Turkey— Aquarius is *Bailgu*, the Brush Fence—Antares the Fire Carrier, *War-roo-boordina*—and Rigel is *Kara* the Red-backed Spider at Orion's right foot.

Orion is *N-yeeru-na* the Hunter, the giant, the coward of the skies. His impotence and shame are the Awful Example and the moral of the man-corroborees. Night after night through eternity he chases the giggling girls of the Pleiades, little desert devils of the *Mingari* girls, to be defied, waylaid and kept forever at bay by *Kambu-gudha*, their elder sister, the V in Taurus, who laughs him to scorn—they double and dodge, throwing the dust into his eyes, mocking him in their jests and songs, sparkling mockery at his rage.

N-yeeru-na, Hunter of Women, but a hunter baffled and shamed by women, in the man-making ceremonies is one of the first great morality plays, an Aboriginal ballet of all the brightest stars in the southern skies. It was for Men Only.

If a woman sees it she will die. In the initiation corroborees Kambu-gudha and the Mingari were acted by young men and boys.

N-yeeru-na dances, his body reddened by lust and fire. In feathers, red-ochre, knotted hair-belt and whitened pubic tassel, the red fire of Betelgeuse his club in his left hand, he beckons and waves to the Mingari girls to come to his camp. Returning home from gathering food, they huddle together and refuse. N-yeeru-na stamps and tramples, he strides them down, his gestures and dances angry and obscene. In fear of him they trip and fall, and tremble, hiding under their gnarled dragon humps, spinning like a swarm of bees in silver clouds of pollen to confuse him—in the brilliant Australian skies at night the Pleiades are many more than seven. Nearer comes N-yeeru-na, threatening, snatching—the girls run—

But Kambu-gudha, elder sister, stands naked before him, her feet and legs wide apart, her left foot Aldebaran filled with fire magic, kicking up a dazzle of light to blind him. She dares him with her whole body in maddening mocking dances, trips him with her yamstick quivering fire, exciting him and flaunting, showing contempt in calling a line of puppies between them—the faint wavy line of stars between Orion and the V in Taurus. Soon he is jeered and laughed at by all the neighbouring stars and constellations—*Jurr-jurr*, Night Owl, Canopus, in his hollow chuckle, *Weeloo* the Curlew screaming, Rigel, *Kara* the Red-backed Spider viciously stinging his prancing feet, *Maalu* and *Kanyala*, the Pointers, pointing derision, till *Babba* the Dingo, Horn of the Bull, flings himself at N-yeeru-na, savagely springs upon him and swings now east, now west, by his pubic tassel, till *Beera*, the comical old Moon, mocks at his shame and failure and all the camps in the sky are ringing with ribald laughter.

I

Kambu-gudha wins! N-yeeru-na's fire grows dim, his guts are gone, his manhood and his fame as a mighty hunter. Pale and wan, he limps away to the west with all the Mingari women, screaming their triumph and scorn, hunting him. His name is shame.

N-yeeru-na corroboree is a comedy or satire before very young initiates, first recited to them, said Mrs Bates, with many unpublishable details till they know it by heart. The boys must look upon all women to be their slaves and do their will in sexual demands at all times and places. A ruthless and savage power is thus instilled. The drama's lesson is the dominance of the male. Myth and performance are both grossly phallic, an orgy corroboree where the women of the tribes, sitting apart as they are in the sky are raided at will by the dancers and all the men to the wild and raucous singing and the thud of a club on the sand, mankind's first drum. The play is presented night after night while ever the giant Orion is striding the skies and the mischievous Pleiades twinkle above.

But in a thousand and one nights my quaint hostess Kabbarli could never relate the tales, with their songs and dances, the world's first operas and the True Australian literature of man's visions and imaginings how many thousand years ago? Some of her legends and fables were continent-wide, some confined to a few square miles with stories told of every bird and tree, every conspicuous star and stone. Of some she had nine or ten versions from varied geographies and tribes. Some were world-wide, closely akin to Old World mythologies that had lived through milennia in the spoken word.

She could tell them much more graphically than she could write, setting the action, character and scene. She was not greaty concerned with literary style, nor was she a "reader".

The tank library was limited indeed, an anachronism even as her dress—a complete set of Dickens, Tennyson's *Collected Poems*, Kipling's *Kim* and *Just So Stories*, a few of Stevenson and Scott, a few best-sellers of Edwardian days, Palgrave's *Golden Treasury*, *The Golden Bough* of Sir James Frazer, Perry's *Children of the Sun*. Of the Australian section Dr Howitt and Dr Roth, Baldwin Spencer, the Leach bird book and the Cayley, were heavily margined and interlined with her additions and contradictions, native names and natural history notes. The Bible of her childhood, Shakespeare, the Gilbert and Sullivan plays, *Pears' Cyclopaedia*, *The Family Doctor*, with *Folklore* and other semi-scientific journals, shared the two flimsy shelves . . . very little to read, but not much time in the day or light in the night for reading, no money to spare for rail freight on library books from the cities, never a bookshop in a million square miles. She had subscribed to a few newspapers that arrived from days to months late.

Coronets were a commonplace in her dusty mail-bag and she had many correspondents from the cities and overseas. A friend who held her in high esteem and frequently published her little studies and stories was Arthur Mee of *The Children's Encyclopaedia*, as also the Adelaide *Chronicle* and the *Western Mail*, Australian weeklies; but since World War I there was little interest in the Aborigines.

As our quest of Minmilla continued, with Daisy's authority and permission I sent the sensational story to the Press—to my regret. Minmilla turned up in the camp next day with a bouncing baby boy in her wooden scoop and with Thannana by the hand—a reformed cannibal, Daisy insisted with much relief, but certainly a mother happy and proud. Minmilla never knew she had a chance of heavy damages in a criminal libel case, but her boy arrived with a barrow-load from Kabbarli's camp of baby clothes for the pale little stranger no more than a day old: two print frocks new and clean, a new billy-can with half a pound of tea, two packets of self-raising flour for johnnie-cakes with a tin of peach jam, two combs, three cakes of yellow soap, two sticks of tobacco, and a tin of boiled sweets—a christening party in the wurley of Home Sweet Home, the baby visibly blackening as his father's son.

Happy ending! No cannibal party and all well. Kabbarli still could boast that never a half-caste was conceived in her camps—the cruel old brand of racial prejudice in "touch of the tar-brush" and "yellow streak", "the virtues of neither and the vices of both", man's inhumanity to his own children through centuries of heartbreak, and a pitiable myopia from which we are only now released. It was useless to argue with her about all the endlessly blended hues of the human complexion in the melting-pot of the world, or about the admirable natures and achievement of Aboriginal Asian and European derivation in Australia, or to quote St Paul: *"He hath made of one blood all nations of men."* She had seen the sorrows, diseases and degradation inflicted on Aboriginal women and their children by the passing stranger, outcasts of the towns inbred in beggary and squalor. The sins of the fathers she visited on the children because she was afraid for them. Their lives she could not share.

With the train from the west I must be gone, bound for Kingoonya and the Dutch mailman, Jacob Santing, three hundred miles north to the opal fields at Coober Pedy, now world-famous, then only a few invisible holes in the hills once under the inland sea, where twenty or thirty opal gougers lived in their burrows, like moles. I was sorry to leave. I realized the immeasurable orbit of her vision of mankind and the need of her loving-kindness to these waifs and strays from the desert sands, her long life's solitary work. She came with me to the siding, the council of the Old Men our bodyguard, my suitcase balanced on Gooinmurdo's head. Good friends, we waved good-bye to meet again. Two pairs of *kurdaitcha* slippers were her parting gift to me, fearsome blood-encrusted things, reeking with emu-fat, crawling with lice, but of gruesome interest to me. As I could not take them till after dehydration and fumigation, she would post them on some day.

My gift to her was delayed till I reached Adelaide—a carefully chosen crateful of all the brightest books of the day, some thirty or forty including, I remember, Bernard Shaw's *The Adventures of the Black Girl in her Search for God*, and *Blood in the Sand*, an Australian novel of the day about a race of Spaniards marooned in the Red Centre, a beautiful blonde heroine and Aboriginal princes and kings orating like Roman senators all over the place. There were many original and valuable books with a hamper of delectable "iron-clads" for the toast and tea: asparagus, whitebait, fruits in syrup, little "one-woman" delicacies. . . .

After a long silence a letter came to me, acknowledging, reproving: she thanked me for the freight duly acknowledged. She had taken the liberty of returning the books to the bookseller immediately for their cash value less per cent, and also the hamper of groceries for the equivalent in flour, sugar, sago, rice, the cheaper jams and preserves, and tea, all for her natives, and for the children a tin of boiled sweets. For these she was abjectly grateful and would ever be, with joyful thanks to me from such as Jinnawillie. She herself was more blessed to give than to receive.

Nine

WHILE I PLODDED across the continent for ten years before the Stuart Highway, battling on mail trucks, on camels threading the ranges, on pack-horses swimming rivers east and west as far as I could go, letters from Daisy told me she longed to be on my tracks to complete her field work. One lyrical screed of forty-seven pages full of joyous underlinings and exclamation marks announced that she had just been awarded the C.B.E., King George V so graciously remembering his good and faithful Kabbarli, so humble and so far. She could have no greater reward. From Thursday Island to Groote Eylandt in 1933 I sailed the Gulf of Carpentaria on the lugger *Noosa*, a thousand miles of crocodile rivers and unin-habited shores, and there, at Roper Bar, watched the natives carry ashore the stores for an Arnhem Land patrol of the Northern Territory police.

Arnhem Land was ultima thule on the Australian map, out of bounds to white men for fifty years or so. Two or three cattle stations and mineral fields of early colonization had been abandoned there from hostility of the blacks. Salt-water tribes of a rich coastal country, as yet untouched by civilization, were of a livelier intelligence, with their arts and crafts, their resentment of the intruder. Their Aboriginal race, in physique, customs, character and languages in temperament and temper, was strongly infiltrated for a century and more by constant invasion of praus from Macassar trading for trepang along the Arafura and Gulf shores. After a few murders and futile punitive raids, they were left to their own devices, the peninsula surveyed by David Lindsay in 1885 as a closed native reserve.

The only news from Arnhem Land was smoke signal of endless tribal wars and rumours sensational in the nineteen-twenties. Two white women, mother and daughter, were alleged to be wandering with the wild tribes, swept ashore from the wreck of the *Douglas Mawson* in 1924. In Caledon Bay in 1925 the lugger *Iolanthe* with blood-stained decks was salvaged by Horace Foster and Bill Harney after the murder of a Japanese crew of five. Two "blow-ins" from Borroloola, beach-combing that fatal strand, vanished in 1929, and in 1930 a wild dog hunter on the western border was waddied to death at Mainoru. Two expeditions, one of Sir Hubert Wilkins, one of Sergeant Bridgland from Borroloola, sailed along the coast but did not stay.

Then came the news in 1931 of seven Japanese from another pearling-lugger massacred in Blue Mud Bay. The sole survivor had walked the coast to Darwin, nearly a year on the way, and for five months of the wet season the police party was delayed. Missionaries at the outposts of Millingimbi and Groote Eylandt complained that the mainlanders in their dug-out canoes with their murders and magics were becoming mischievous and troublesome. The shore of oblivion must be brought within the long arm of the law. Four young police constables from Darwin, M.Cs. Morey, Mahoney, Hall and

McColl, with their trackers and camp equipment including a boat bound for Blue Mud Bay and Caledon Bay, rode north from Roper Bar in the name of G.R.

Into the "tiger country" I watched them ride away. As I semi-circled the continent again by air, Burketown to Perth, news came that McColl had been fatally speared by an Arnhemlander named Tuckiar at Woodah Island in Blue Mud Bay. The police party returned to Darwin in due course with the guilty tribesmen on both counts, convicted in Darwin Supreme Court by witnesses and interpreters, death sentences commuted to life imprisonment in the jail at Fannie Bay. A month or two later, Tuckiar ran away but never reached his country, shot by a police trooper while resisting arrest.

There was an outcry in the Southern press for and against the Arnhemlanders, deploring man-hunts and police raids as provocative, trials of the natives in British courts without knowledge of law and language a travesty of justice, and demanding that overtures of peace be made to reclaim a wilderness for the protection of white and black.

An ambassador was called for, a friend of the Aborigines, one they would trust and welcome among them, to break down the barriers and pave the way. First choice, to her delight and my amazement, was Mrs Daisy Bates.

She wrote in glee that she was called to Canberra for preliminaries, arrangements, discussions of ways and means, that her whole life's work had been a preparation for missions and commissions such as these. At seventy-four years old she was confident and courageous, dramatizing herself in dreams. She would travel alone into the heart of darkness, disarm the wild men of their wackaburras and spears, make friends with the whole of Arnhem Land, new worlds to conquer for the King and Queen, deeds that won the Empire.

A guest at Government House in Canberra, she conferred with the Prime Minister and his Cabinet, addressed professors and senators, was interviewed, féted and entertained, a distinct social success. She went sight-seeing in blizzards, lofted her skirts à la Bopeep and danced up the marble staircases to show her ability and verve, "flirted" with the elder statesmen, amused them all with her quiddities and quips, her airy bandinage . . . but alas for her embassy to the Arnhemlanders, her visions of herself as grandmother and spiritual guide to the wild-haired sons of the Bugis with their seventeen-barb spears. The political powers-that-were wagged their heads hopelessly. No doubt they expected a madonna, or a ministering angel, or a mystic like Rider Haggard's "She". Lavender and Old Lace, Quality Street, they all agreed would be sadly out of place at piccaninny daylight alone in the grisly blue mud of Blue Mud Bay. Daisy never knew why they abruptly told her good-bye and booked her back to Ooldea with a Commonwealth grant of £4 a week.

Dr Donald Thomson was appointed in her stead, a brilliant young anthropologist from Melbourne University who camped and rambled for three years with Remburunga, Ritherunga, and coastal tribes to the north and west in a last stronghold of the Stone Age in invaluable research, first steps in colonization of a region in Australia of immense natural wealth and in friendship with its people now much the same as all the rest.

Kabbarli returned to her tent in the brush crestfallen but patient in her work. I travelled in 1934 north-about from Fremantle the whole coast of Western Australia and all its "isles adjacent" in the yacht *Silver Gull* of Captain J. R.

Grey, R.N.R., with Mrs Beatrice Grey, F.L.S., and a crew of Perth Sea Scouts, under the Blue Ensign as a ship of discovery collecting navigational knowledge for the Admiralty, marine zoology data and specimens for the Linnaean Society and British Museum. I was still and ever collecting knowledge and stories of Australia for books, the Press, and magazines. Returning to Adelaide, I became a member of the *Advertiser* staff as a feature writer for the next four years.

In 1935 there was a withering drought inland in South Australia, and merciless heat, at Ooldea 120 degrees in the shade, no shade. A letter came from Mrs Bates that bush-fires were raging in the scrub all round her, that her natives from their scorched rags and ashes had fled to Cook and Wynbring. Jinnewillee and Jilganya, the last old man of Yuldilgabbi, died. No one was left in the camps. She must walk twice a day to the siding, four miles, through the smouldering bush for her small ration of water, needing always more to put out the encroaching fires. She was digging holes in the ground to bury her precious notes, but her sight was failing from sandy blight.

She wrote again that twice the railway men from the siding had saved her camp by cutting fire-breaks and beating back the flames that now threatened not only her life's work but her life. But the men were urgently defending their own little homes and government property. The sleepers of the line caught fire. They were working day and night. She could not send for them except in imminent danger. Her notes and manuscripts from all the years were in the flimsy and inflammable tent and bough shades. She could not leave them—they were packed to vacate. The hot winds carried sparks, the brush fence was often alight when she was alone at night. She thrashed it out with branches, stamped it into the ground, stifled it with buckets of sand—

Here a sentence in her letter gave me a fright.

"I am so blind that I can only smell the burning when my clothes are on fire."

I read no further. This was no time for sweet sympathy in telegrams or fragrant gifts and fans. How could I help her in a crisis over seven hundred miles? With Sir Lloyd Dumas, managing director of the *Advertiser*, I asked for an immediate interview, the letter in my hand. I told him of her pitiable plight, of her gentle and generous nature, of her courage and patience, her super-human self-denial and independence, her self-immolation for her ideal. Above all I stressed the value of her collections of data from the now-vanished Aboriginal tribes, and the grievous loss to Australia if they should be destroyed. She alone could explain and interpret her thousands of notes of unfamiliar sequences, languages, legends, that must be saved. The story of her life could be told by her alone. At her age there was no time to lose. With the bushfires, I was alarmed lest we should be too late. I remember I ended the heartfelt little harangue with a prophecy that came true.

"When she's dead," I told him, "they'll set up a monument at Ooldea to the memory of her terrible years alone. If they're going to be worthwhile, now is the time."

Sir Lloyd Dumas listened quietly with his characteristic kindness and quick perception of practical ways and means. He instantly suggested that Mrs Bates and her manuscripts be brought to Adelaide by the *Advertiser* as soon as possible for later decisions to be made. He knew of the little lady, held her in high esteem. His editors regretted that her writings, especially in recent years, were diffuse, profuse, rambling, too mannered and out of date or too obscure in meaning for the present day, sometimes involved with aboriginal words and references unexplained, sometimes juvenile as in fairy tale. Her life story certainly could be of interest, but how could she cope with autobiography if health and sight were failing?

I offered to be the ghost in this very unusual case, and without any further parley he agreed. For Australasian syndicate rights in newspaper serial of the life story, the *Advertiser*, if I remember correctly, offered £500 to be paid in advance, with transport arranged and all facilities provided for the work in Adelaide.

I hurried away to the post office to wire her the wonderful news of help, hope and relief: "Terms in letter following, please advise." A fortnight later I was nonplussed to receive a gracious but non-committal reply. Would I convey a thousand deeply grateful thanks to Sir Lloyd Dumas in his offer superlatively kind of terms so fabulously high, but she was not at liberty at present to accept. A gentle rain from heaven had fallen at Ooldea, dousing the bushfires. Her natives were back, needing her guidance and care. The crisis was over for the time being. With regard to the future, she had several times approached the Prime Minister outlining ideas to carry her work farther afield with government authority and sponsorship. She visioned an appointment as High Commissioner, as it were, to the Aboriginal people throughout Australia, with administrative and judicial powers to alleviate their sorrows and guide their destinies to freedom and peace. She would travel, throughout the Commonwealth, the Oracle, the ever-Bountiful, leading the leaderless race and nation of the True Australians in a hard and cruel world where they had survived too long.

Pleasant letters of genuine interest she had received from the Right Honourable J. A. Lyons, then Prime Minister; no definite promise as yet. It was announced he would soon be crossing by the Transcontinental to Perth. She had written requesting a personal interview to discuss a preliminary appointment as Protector-in-General. Gladly would she have accepted the *Advertiser*'s offer were it not for her "gentleman's agreement" with the Prime Minister and her loyalty to her natives. In other words, she had an appointment in the Stone Age.

It was a very long letter, essentially to be shown to Sir Lloyd Dumas who made no comment but seemed relieved. They had found the little lady a prickle-bush now and then. However, he agreed to leave the matter open until a definite refusal should be received.

Another longer letter followed . . . from the Valley of Humiliation, desolation and despair. The Prime Minister, passing Ooldea in the drowsy heat of afternoon, was asleep. His secretary declined to wake him. The little Dresden figure waited in vain, in full view of the train. Under the royal umbrella and through the gossamer veil her cheeks burned pink with embarrassment and shame.

"*De profundis*", she wrote. "Oh, my dear, such a cruel contempt, before all those Philistines the snub direct! Some were laughing, I'm sure they must have known. I had brought some special native magics as a gift and vitally interesting letters and reports with a prospectus of all my aims and objects, present, future, past. I was laden down with ceremonial spears and letter-sticks and photographs and folios, anticipating a special interview, an audience, don't you know? In all my best gigglywinks! I felt such a fool standing there speechless, not knowing which way to turn, till I begged the guard to leave me the key of the lamp room, and there I hid till it was dark. I confided in no one, but the fettlers at the siding must have known, I was so

137

distraught. I have once or twice before knocked at the gates of government in vain, and I never shall do it again. . . . My brightest hopes are gone, my own resources completely exhausted, my allowance too small for me to do anything at all. . . ."

Again I wrote, urging acceptance of the *Advertiser* contract, a respite and refreshment in the city's comforts and companionship, for the case of her present health and future work, for records of the past a national need. Friends were awaiting her in Adelaide.

The reply came that I was hoping for, a gay and childlike change of mood. She was packing the gigglywinks and would be with us before long. The policemen at Cook and Tarcoola were taking over her natives for rations and jobs, so they would not be in want.

"Please arrange for my accommodation at the South Australian Hotel and later the Queen Adelaide Club," she wrote. "I never could tolerate half measures. I've been as poor as wood so long that now I shall revel in the best, only the best. And rent for me an office in the Commonwealth Bank, a convenient one for work, and meeting friends, and interviews. We're having a wonderful feast for all camps when the cheque arrives—such a surprise for my bank so faithful to me in these cheese-paring years. . . . The *mourra* gods are auspicious, the weather is cool. . . . I'll be with you in a week or two. . . ."

Ten

S O THE GOLDEN BOUGH of the life's work was saved. The day came when the battered trunks, dress-baskets and bundles were trundled off in the barrow to be labelled Adelaide. The tent, library tank, cans, pannikins, blankets, towels and "gigglywinks" of Home Sweet Home were a grand hand-out to the natives with all the money she could spare. Farewell from Ooldea siding, the ragged camps assembled, bodyguard of the tribal elders with their cockatoo crests and mud curls. Their Kabbarli leant from a carriage window with a last "Be good!" and "Come back soon!" in Meerikoogada language as the crowded train pulled out— a front-page story with photographs for the southern Press of Australia, photographers and reporters on the scene. Goodbye to the Dreaming! Kilmeny was coming back to her own people, never to live in the Stone Age again.

On the night she arrived I wrote for the morning paper a leader-page special of welcome, announcing the forthcoming serial and book. Mrs Rymill, president of the National Council of Women, came with me to meet the train, our arms full of roses and freesias, lavender, sweet peas, all the most fragrant English flowers for a desert wayfarer from the heat and hard labour reprieved.

Hugs and loving greetings, she was in high spirits, dancing as we crossed the street to the South Australian Hotel, received as a Very Important Person by proprietors and commissionaires. A boy selling violets in the vestibule, sensing a birthday or a gala, offered his own wares. Daisy, to our dismay, dumped on the urchin's head, to the last bud and branch, our specially chosen flowers.

"Take these, too, and sell them, you darling little man!" she beamed, leaving us not a twig, not a sprig, for her room, where wonders awaited an exile from the sand.

Carpets and shaded lights, easy-chairs, writing-desk, telephone—from herself in the mirror she darted back with apologies, and then hearty laughter. "My dears! I didn't know me! I haven't seen myself in years. Goodness gracious, what a fright I am!"

The bathroom was fairyland, nickel taps running hot and cold, the shower showering down. She turned them all on with a wild surmise, turned them off in horror of waste, turned them on again with a radiant smile.

"Oh, that sound! That heavenly music of water flowing! I could listen for ever. How much are we allowed? Would they mind if I fill it up to the top just once in my life and sit there and *wallow* with that blessed water up to my chin for hours?"

With the mischievous delight of a guilty child she was turning it on and off when we left her . . . to the strange adventure of a city at night, voices and noises around her, jangle and roar in a mad square mile of the traffic and the crowds, moving mazes of the coloured lights. She sat by the window watching the neon signs, the deathless army squadding the intersections, hearing the post office clock's West-

140

minster chimes till midnight tolled and the streets were quiet, Adelaide's half million home to sleep. Her room was bright as Ooldea moonlight, no bushfires, no dingo howls.

Her first thought next morning was to pay her respects at Government House, signing the visitors' book, then to the *Advertiser* to meet the editors and managing director, Sir Lloyd Dumas. She expressed her grateful thanks on a gay social occasion—the Woman from the Dreaming could never be businesslike. Nothing was questioned, no conditions or contract were required in "a gentlemen's agreement", and a bottomless well of well-being at the bank.

Method and manner of writing the newspaper serial and the book were left to me. My work, both journalistic and a book of my own, were set aside for the time being. Her hundredweight of copious notes was delivered to the *Advertiser* library for us to classify and thread like beads on a string the years and chapters of her life. It was feet deep of jigsaw puzzle, knowledge new to the world, often with Aboriginal words and vocabularies, rituals, racial links, that no one but Daisy could elucidate: for an old lady of seventy-six a labour of Hercules, and she had tried and tried—but well she knew the scenes and sequences of her pilgrimage through all the western tribes, and we could set our chronoligies by these. The incidental archaeologies and anthropologies for her books, we sifted and set aside.

Most of her diaries petered out in the first months of the years of heat and stress, flood and drought, pressure of work, lack of materials. They became a frenzied jotting of miscellaneous reminders and researches. Her published writings were comparatively few, as she was often far out of touch with the newspapers or magazines in which they appeared. There was a love story or two written around tribal relationships or rites, there were child studies, sensitive character sketches in tragedy or comedy, crusades in cuttings from the Press, and contributions to historical and geographical proceedings and scientific journals. Her one and only published poem, a faded floweret from her mid-Victorian girlhood of which she was shyly proud, she had kept through all the years.

None of the writings was recent. Though a fluent and graphic speaker, a literally voluminous correspondent, the trend of the age, the discipline and dove-tailing of brevities in free-lancing, the manual labour of typewriting and editors regretting that space did not permit, she found too depressing. We decided that she would talk, and I would write, and she would read for additions and amendments, and I would make "fair copy" of the work with these for her finalities.

"Your name," she said, "must be on the title-page with mine."

I said, "Wait till it's finished, and we'll see."

She had chosen her own title, *My Natives and I*, and her publisher, John Murray of London, whom she had met. She was duly installed in the library, with all her "gigglywinks" round her, and the work began. The morning was given to the interviews, natural conversation of events, impressions, people, flash-backs and the Aboriginalities as they came to mind. My knowledge of all her regions from Beagle Bay to Fowler's Bay, from Kimberley to Ooldea via the Ophthalmia Range and south-central Australia to Nullarbor Plain, also my respect and affection for the natives and knowledge of tribes continent-wide, were invaluable to me and plain sailing for her—biography without tears. I jotted down everything in shorthand and set it in sequence of time for chapter and verse, not forgetting highlights for newspaper serial. Quickly we skimmed the distance. I was careful, and

142

she would have wished it, that all material of the book was exclusively hers, only the paraphrasing, the actual writing and the arrangement mine.

Announcement of her arrival kindled a lively interest and she had many friends in Adelaide, a city that honours conventional idealism and pities the poor Aborigines, its own sins against them in the far past. The nun-like figure sedately pacing in King William Street was immediately recognized. Her visitors ranged through bishops, professors, school teachers, club presidents with invitations to "speak", station owners, missionaries, motherly women with home-made cakes or eager to do her washing, and little boys and girls for autographs.

"Page-ing Mrs Daisy Bates!" the house-phones at the South Australian were carolling all day, flowers, letters, notes, to be delivered. The rigid reserve forgotten, she was the friend of all the world, inviting it to luncheon, dinner and tea. Greeting a dozen at a time, she mustered them all to the dining-room at the bang of the gong. Her own menu was frugal but she tried to insist on the best for the guests from *hors d'œuvres* to liqueurs.

"My hotel bill for the first week is £37," she confessed to me in fright. "Isn't that shameful of me . . . but so many wonderful friends and so many beautiful things to eat after so many years of nobody but me on stale bread and tea!"

By our *Advertiser* staff her endless invitations were firmly refused. Fish, fruit and coffee with "lashings" of cream were her choice as a rule. Though she was never anti-alcohol, except among the natives, I never knew her to raise a festive glass even in a toast to the king. Tea was her stimulus and pleasure any time of day from the first cup she made for herself at piccaninny daylight.

She was always an early riser, reading the morning papers

143

through her magnifying glass and later thoughtfully discussing the news of the day, political news especially. A confirmed little conservative and a good Anglican, she attended the cathedral most Sundays, whisked off to dinner and motoring tours by bevies of friends with whom she was quite unreserved, entertaining and gay. Her favourite occupations were shopping for toys for their children, also hampers and parcels for the natives, cartons of "iron-clads" —bully beef, jams, tinned fruit—packets of flour, tea, sugar in bags, boiled sweets, addressed "Dooroomagum, Ooldea, S.A." or "Yalli-Yalli and Dhambilnga (known as Big Nellie and Paddy Bon Bon). Try Cook or Tarcoola."

In some ways as much an anachronism in mind as in dress, she refused to speak on the telephone, had never attended the movies, and to the radios—even those bellowing along the street—she turned a deaf ear.

"Oh dear, those coarse voices!" or "Tell me, is that what they really call music nowadays?"

She delighted in the work at the *Advertiser*—back to the wheel of the world, from sun-time to the urgency of the ticking clock, from the void and silence of the bush to the perpetual sound and motion of a city newspaper. For the first time in twenty years money was jingling in her purse, money that she had earned, and all the shop-windows in glittering array tempting her to buy a thousand things she didn't want and give them all away. It made her feel young again, a woman of affairs.

She was in to the office every day on the tick of half past nine, beaming to Miss Adams, the librarian, leading her a merry dance of letters to post, friends to ring up, flowers to buy, to arrange, to present, notes to deliver, lunches to order, gifts to send. Miss Adams, a quiet senior girl accustomed to uneventful days, collapsed with locomotor ataxia or shingles, she told me, from dancing attendance on the Blithe Spirit and trying to catch up with her.

Daisy spent the morning reading through copy, my type-written copy from yesterday recalling memories in reams. Her pencil never altered or modified a phrase. Once or twice a week there were flittings-out to luncheons to "speak" at various clubs or circles, or to be hostess or guest of honour at afternoon teas. Far from being recluse or reserved, she was always vivacious, with an almost vice-regal graciousness and verve, warmly interested in other people's endless varieties of vocations and good works as they appreciated hers. She loved being interviewed, photographed.

Walking on air, dignity and benignity threading the throng, she loved to be recognized and hailed by those who approach celebrities everywhere. If not, she would introduce herself, to the lift girl wafting her high and low—how exciting!—to the florist selling her primroses—childhood memories long ago. With a fine disregard of mere money she would invariably hand her purse to the waitress or the bus-conductor, with "Take whatever you need", in implicit trust looking the other way while they, somewhat startled, extracted shillings and pence from a roll of notes. The taxi-man and the hall porter went their way rejoicing, the waiter found a token under the plate. The hungry years forgotten, the last shilling would be given away—for the *pourboire*. *Noblesse oblige*, don't you know?

I had written the Commonwealth Government on her behalf that the grant of £4 a week awarded her with the C.B.E. a few years before was an estimation very low in the high cost of living and the value of her present work. An advance to £6 a week was announced in the Press. She was suitably grateful but ironic.

"How munificent! How magnamimous they are! Six

shillings a day more, two guineas a week. Ah well, it will cover my tips."

The famous little figure, proudly erect, never changed, but her wardrobe was refreshed. Collars and cuffs, toques, ties, veils, gloves, shoes, in Everywoman's delight of shopping in Temptation Row, were replaced by new. Dyers, invisible menders and renovaters tinted and trimmed the frayed and faded suits and coatees, resurrected the neat little jockey jackets and nine-gored skirts, the leg-of-mutton sleeves, while millinery magic redeemed the perished ribbons and flowers of the turn-of-the-century hats.

King George's umbrella, in full sail, gyrated at levies and garden parties on the lawns at Government House where its owner was still and ever a welcome guest among the intelligentsia, for her singular personality no less than her knowledge, her eloquence, her empire loyalties and one-woman crusade. Perhaps from her secret dreams of grandeur, the royalties, vice-royalties and peeresses and peers in general were "my own people". They found her, to their amazement, even exquisitely feminine, highly amusing, facetious as one of themselves. Her precise protocol suddenly sparkled off into mid-Victorian gaiety and mischievous Irish wit, dated but infectious, followed by abject apologies—

"Oh, but I'm incorrigible! A flibbertigibbet, don't you know? Do please forgive me" . . . a long guilty face and a dainty square of Limerick lace brushing away tears of laughter.

The mellow Irish voice, in tales of the bush or vignettes of the natives, could hold the dinner-table or the drawing-room enthralled. She loved to be the pivot of attention, and to warn the "grave and reverend seigneurs"—generals, premiers, professors—till she was eighty that she was "a heartless flirt". If she felt she was ignored, or if the party bored her, regardless of etiquette she would slip away and leave for home.

In the ease, comfort, friendliness, of Adelaide's happy living her health and sight improved, her step was brisk—a boisterous hoyden running up the stairs. Good nourishing food, a temperate climate, friends, leisure, relief from labour and cares, lightened the burden of the years. Her face was smooth as a girl's, neither wrinkled nor tanned, her eyes clear blue and without spectacles, hair simply-coiled, not grey but silver-fair. Cosmetics meant less to her than fashions. I never knew her to complain of the influenzas, colds or hyperchondrias, or to attend a doctor with either slight or serious ills. Mentally, physically, her stamina was amazing, her independence admirable to the end.

She had changed her residence from the South Australian Hotel to the Queen Adelaide Club, the sacred social precints of the "Adeladies" where she loved to dwell, and from there to the Stirling Hotel in the "dress circle" of the Mount Lofty hills, walking miles through hawthorn lanes and rhododendrons at the week-ends. She tried in vain to unearth a side-saddle, to take up riding again.

During a visit of the Duke of Gloucester she was "bidden" to dance at the ball. The city en fête with coloured lights and bunting, the famous Adelaide Greys of the mounted police prancing and curvetting through cheering crowds and a "regular right-down royal prince" heading the procession from a flood-lit Rolls Royce to the flood-lit Town Hall, moved her to tears of emotion that she should live to see the heart-felt loyalties of world's end Australians for a son of England's king, strangely closer to her in thought than a son of her own. Proudly she wore her order and chevron of the C.B.E. among the medals and honours of the nation-builders.

"I was greatly relieved," she said, "that His Highness did not ask me to dance. Of course I must have consented, but nobody nowadays knows the schottische and mazurka, and the waltz is so much changed, and the polka wouldn't do at all!"

In her evening dress she was a period-piece for *Lady Windermere's Fan*—the wasp-waist white satins brocaded with chantilly lace softly framing the heirloom miniature four hundred years old, size three white satin slippers with bows, silk mittens . . . there is a night I remember when friends had taken her to the de Basil Ballet, *Les Sylphides*, *Petrushka*, *Aurora's Wedding*, delights out of this world to one who had lived through thirty years of corroboree, skeleton men bouncing, snake men writhing, black feet thudding in the sand.

A zealous missionary lady had moved in at Ooldea. She gathered the strays of the line, myalls from the Great Sandy, half-castes octoroons, any troop or tribe, marshalled them to school or Sunday school and, calling to the cities for subscriptions and cast-off clothing, began to remodel their lives. She sternly disapproved of Kabbarli's Aboriginal policies, as Kabbarli did of hers, and as most missionaries did of each other. Meeting Daisy in the street, she told of her unbounded success in Christianizing, civilizing, educating, saving souls.

Eagerly Daisy inquired of her old friends, Dhalberdiggin, Dooroomagum, Ngan-nauera. Had they received the hampers she sent? Did they ever remember Kabbarli as she remembered them? What "new mobs" from the desert had arrived?

The missionary lady knew of no such names or tribes. The Christians in her camp were all baptized, Billies and Minnies, Browns, Robinsons, Jones, or by their godfathers' names. They had quite forgotten the bad old heathen days, now singing Moody and Sankey hymns, reading their Bibles, climbing up the golden stair to paradise.

"They're Saved, Mrs Bates," she said reproachfully. "*Saved!*"

Daisy told me of the meeting. "I was speechless," she said. "What could I say? *I bowed.*"

One day King George's umbrella, gipsying to windward across Victoria Square, was hauled back by the traffic cop taking the names of jay-walkers for a £5 fine.

"Mrs Daisy Bates, Queen Adelaide Club", in grave and dulcet tones, was innocence personified. "Dear me, Officer, have I broken the law? My sincerest regrets! So long a nomad in the wilderness, don't you know? No traffic, no regulations, in ten thousand years out there. But I've read of jay-walking. Tell me, is it derived from jay, the bird, or J the letter? I'll never offend again when I know."

Officer was clean bowled. He scratched out her name in his little black book and drew parallelograms for her in the traffic jam. From then on he was her personal friend and guide.

She was the bright particular star of the intersection, where so many waylaid her for autographs and anecdotes, old men out of the park, schoolboys going home from school. She was courteous to all, with special affection for the *Advertiser* staff. When Christmas was coming she insisted on a party of her own in the library, invitations by and large from the "father of the chapel" to Monty the liftman and the copy boys—highly diverting for the shopping crowds the "little old lady passing by", proud as the Queen of Hearts with Knaves from the nearest delicatessen following in her wake with trays of crockery, teapots, sausage rolls and greasy-creamy split-level Kitchener buns in place of the tarts. They right-angled King William Street like the Grand Fleet in line ahead at a review off Cowes. Jaded journalists and hard-shell reporters joined in the fun, and "a good time was had".

A taxi full of gifts for everyone arrived on Christmas Eve, with chocolates, flowers—a gold watch for Miss Adams, one with a sprinkle of diamonds for me, sternly declined. Her endless giving was prodigal and sad. I asked, in its stead, a few brief written lines acknowledging our work together. These, in the years to come, if the book was a success and brought all the happiness I wished for her, would mean much more to me.

Some months later the letter that follows duly arrived. It is here published for the first time, the original treasured by me:

The Advertiser,
ADELAIDE.
30-4-'36

Dear Ernestine Hill,

Now that the book which you kindly and generously helped me with has finally passed on to its fate, I must write to thank you for all you have done and have been to me in its preparation.

As I read through the chapters, I come upon so many evidences of your own words and sentences—the loving-kindnesses and the beautiful way in which you gave of your own genius to its expressions—that I shall always look upon the completed work as as much yours as mine.

Let me thank you for those happy months of col-laboration and the joyousness of our association throughout.

Yours very sincerely,
DAISY M. BATES.

150

Under Daisy's title, *My Natives and I*, the serial commenced publication in the *Advertiser*, in full as I had written it, and was syndicated to the Melbourne *Herald*, Sydney *Sun*, the Brisbane *Courier-Mail* and the *West Australian*, published in full or in episodic form, with photographs. Although the *Advertiser* had bought Australasian rights for syndicated sale and at a generous estimate, Sir Lloyd Dumas and his directors, in an exceptional kindness, now passed on to the little lady's bank account all payments from inter-state, possibly doubling her receipts. She was so "unfinancially minded", as she would say, that I doubt she knew or noted the special consideration—"while there's some there's plenty" where money was concerned, and mainly to give away—but she was radiantly thankful and appreciative to all for all. The newspaper publication brought her a shower of letters and praise from all over Australia, though by the anthropologists, now in steadily increasing numbers in the universities, a few brickbats were thrown. Her allegations of widespread cannibalism, her mournful requiem for the dying race—which applied only to the full-blood and truly tribal—her prejudice, her intolerance of the half-caste, of the full-blood tribes being mixed up together on missions and stations as well as the cross-breed of Asian or European fathers, were deplored and decried. Many a time I suggested to her that her sweeping statements were unjust and unkind. The Old People, totemic, nomadic, primitive paleolithic, beyond the twentieth century in the colonization of Australia had no hope to survive. Their great grandchildren, now to the seventh generation removed from tribal life, were a new and significant hybrid race of populations rapidly rising, an intelligent, useful and estimable race in their own age. These she refused to recognize. In her old-fashioned fetish of birth and breeding, her discriminations were as rigid as those of the tribe, and to her they were not Aborigines but "aboriginese". Distastefully she would pass them by.

From the West came a few repercussions, denials of light-hearted statements and too-vivid pictures of places and people in the bad old days. Glen Carrick, the station she pioneered in the Ophthalmia Range could not be found on the stock map, but as Mount Governor I later identified this when travelling in the region. She and her husband, not Daisy alone, were well remembered at Roy Hill near by, at the de Grey station, Mundabullangana, by the Mackays, all over the Roebourne tablelands by the Withnells and McCraes, and from Broome to Port Hedland down the Eighty Mile Beach of the droving trip. Kimberley ringers laughed at the idea of a lady boss drover in a camp of eight men. Veterans of the stations who were young in those years told merry tales of her "cracking the whip" for clean shirts, daily shaves, polished boots and gentlemanly be-haviour in the mustering camps, her own baths in all the billabongs with washing hung on the anthills to dry, and her "anthropologizing with every Bing-hi on the route". Jack Bates was the pathfinder and the pioneer, his wife was a "first-class passenger", they said. ". . . but a double-bed swag in camp behind a mob of bullocks was hard going for a lady then."

Of her private life I had asked no questions, writing only what she wished to write. She was a woman of high principles with a contempt for lies. In all my travels and knowledge of Australia in a lifetime's researches, with the exception of cannibalism practised by the Aborigines either in hunger or in rite—many times rumoured but never proved—I know of none of her statements that can be flatly denied.

152

Three or four years after our writing of the book, a letter came to me from Western Australia that in Mullewa Hospital Jack Bates, husband of Mrs Daisy Bates, had recently died. He had asked his friend to send me the news—surely to notify his wife? I sent her the letter. To this she made no reply, but asked me a little later would I help her to find Arnold, her only child, whom she had not seen or heard of for many years. She thought he was somewhere in Australia or New Zealand, an A.I.F. captain "shell-shocked" in World War I, invalided home, married, with two, or was it three?, children. They would have told her if he was dead. Arnold must know she was growing very old.

So I tried to find Arnold, over a period of years writing to Army pensions lists, repatriation departments, returned soldiers' and Legacy Clubs, the High Commissioner in New Zealand, Anzac records there, telephone books, electoral rolls —in vain. Nothing remained but inquiries through the police or to advertise in the Press for Missing Friends.

"Please, no," she said firmly. "We wouldn't like either of those. Don't you think he could easily find me when my book appears? I do hope he will."

Not long after the serial publication of *My Natives and I*, I was commissioned, for the jubilee celebrations of Murray Valley irrigation colonies in Australia, to travel the big river and write *Water Into Gold*, the history of the Chaffey Brothers' foundations and the first fifty years of the industry, a spectacular reclamation of so-called "desert" leading to the applied science of irrigation continent-wide. Before Daisy's book could be sent to the London publishers I had to leave Adelaide, and in the following year returned to Melbourne and Sydney for the Matthew Flinders book, *My Love Must Wait*. I was reassured that Mr Max Lamshed, one of the literary editors of the *Advertiser* was acting as editor and agent for Mrs Bates.

To my surprise, when the book appeared as *The Passing of the Aborigines* it was shorn of the earlier chapters, and of her life story very little appeared. I was informed that the publishers decided to concentrate on the dominant interest of Aboriginal life. It was hailed as a worthy little book, winning excellent reviews in England and Australia and steady sales through several editions over thirty years, the latest edition in 1968, paperback, and I hear quickly sold out. No public acknowledgments ever were made to me, or claimed—it would not occur to Mrs Bates that they were customary—except that on many occasions she introduced me to her acquaintances as "my dearest friend—she wrote my book!" Who received publishers' royalties after her death I have never known, nor was I curious to know. My collaboration in the book was a gift to her from me, in recognition of her patient years of devotion to her own ideals and to the people and the land we both knew and loved. Though she lived for fifteen years after publication, closely in touch with critics, societies, historians, anthropological associations and authorities in native affairs in Canberra and Adelaide, and though she re-read it innumerable times, she made no amendments or corrections that I know. She sent me the good reviews with the delight of a happy child.

She was always a good correspondent, from the wilderness wherever possible—pads and candles, ink-bottles full of moths and white ants, dust-storms and floods and mail-trucks permitting. She would toss off thirty-forty pages, fluent and friendly, informative or affectionate, always in handwriting, dancing along in a natural gaiety of exclamation marks and underlinings. These bulky bundles of random observations and emotional outpourings where nothing ever happened no doubt kept her sane in the solitary confinement of the great wide spaces, peopled the silent night with ghostly friends. Their cabinets and cabin trunks were bursting at the seams with her memoirs and reflections . . . but it was hard for them to find the needles in the haystacks of all those years and few had been preserved.

Now the book netted for her reams of correspondence from round the world, inquiries, invitations, appreciations, official and unofficial memos from editors, professors, philanthropists, authors, missions, society leaders, celebrity signatures, and new and true friends from London and overseas.

The light in her hotel window late at night in Adelaide reminded me of the light in the tent at Ooldea . . . Eucla . . . Maamba . . . Wiluna . . . all the way back to Broome. There she was still writing, still alone.

The Commonwealth Government, seeing overseas reviews of the book, discussed an intention of sending her on a lecture tour of America, England and perhaps the Continent, success assured in her unique personality, her life studies of the natives, her originality, sincerity, her beautiful and expressive voice, and the "star quality" that sets her on the front page even yet—that enthrals an artist, an actress, of the magnitude of Katharine Hepburn, a fixed star in perpetual radiation, to bring Daisy May to life again.

I was asked, if this overseas tour could be arranged, would I go with her as "lieutenant", as lady's companion, convener, public relations, as a buffer against the world for her seventy-seven years. Much as I wished it for her, I declined. I was tethered by family ties, deep in research for the Flinders book, having circled Australia by ship in his wake, and I had neither the talent nor the temperament for public life.

But in any case the vulture-shadows of War were very soon over the world again.

Eleven

AUSTRALIA was Kabbarli's country.

She never expressed a wish or a need to return to England and Ireland. Sister Kathleen was dead and her only daughter, Violet, in Buenos Aires. She and Daisy exchanged loving letters every now and again; she read them out to me with family pride. Violet, no doubt, pictured her roving aunt as a Boadicea riding among Red Indian gauchos and caballeros over the pampas or in an adobe hut by an Orinoco's side.

Sixty-two years are a long time to be acclimatized. Though her vivid memories and valued friendships might have called, though her welcome and welfare were assured in England, her life's work was her reason for being, even at seventy-five—still so much to be done in collating and compiling, her promise to the natives to come back, then new horizons—to cover the continent, to know its own people in the "untravell'd world" where they still roamed, and as it was in the beginning.

She wanted to learn and lead. She still and ever visioned herself as a Mrs Sanders of the River, a precursor and pathfinder to the "King's Man", who would be a Lawrence of Arabia, or a British Raj or another India, to deliver to him the keys of the kingdom, a continent at peace.

She was acutely conscious of colour-line, detested the idea of assimilation, integration, the policies of governments and missions in favour of miscegenation, the in-breeding with European and Asian and early-as-possible breeding out in education and regimentation of the favoured race of Australians in the miracle survival of fossil Man. She deplored the mass-production monotony of "shibboleths" such as civilization, the One World, Esperanto . . . delighted in languages as the expression of country . . . dreamed up for the Aboriginal tribes still in existence their rightful possession of all their realms and regions under one benign autocracy without confusion of parliaments or parties. She knew she was a century late.

A Commonwealth Census in the nineteen thirties estimating Aboriginal populations of the various States, including hybrid, half-caste, quadroon, even octoroon under certain circumstances as Aborigines without civic rights "within the meaning of the Act", reported some 60,000 in the Territory and the West, rapidly dwindling to mere hundreds in the Eastern States, and finally in the Australian Capital Territory, Canberra, "Aborigines, 1". The mystery man intrigued Mrs Daisy Bates. Who was he? His totem? His country? His tribe?

"I'm writing to the Prime Minister," she told me, "asking the permission of Honourable Members to set up my tent on Lake Burley Griffin and establish my camp. This single solitary man may well be an emissary from Arnhem Land or some such, seeking a charter for his people, or the last lone survivor of a Canberra tribe. But the idea is a splendid one. I would be pleased to nominate a council from my natives everywhere, with direct approach to the government in Aboriginal affairs from this time on. They will need me as their interpreter and guide, to protect them from this socialist propaganda and sedition, don't you know? I could address them in their own languages, and formulate the agenda, and we would deal with problems as they arise. Now, my dear, will you also write, and join forces with me in plans and recommendations until we get the tribunal going and see where we are?"

Runnymede on the Molonglo River, *kurdaitcha* slippers parked with the galoshes and top hats of the V.I.Ps, were too fanciful for me. The letter was acknowledged courteously for future deliberation—the Institute of Aboriginal Affairs of today, but a vastly different "personnel". How Mrs Bates reconciled the ideals with the pitiful truth as she knew it, her anthems with her elegies, I do not know, but she never wavered. The divine right of England's kings was the mainspring of her life—more, they were enthroned in her heart.

At the death of George V she slowly paced King William Street in the dismal black of deep mourning, black-veiled, black-gloved, black-shod, the black royal umbrella a canopy at the intersections . . . confounding Adelaide. For days she was in retreat and pale with grief. Her voice was reverently lowered.

The abdication of Edward VIII, which too soon followed, seared her to the heart. She haughtily refused to believe it. Her king could do no wrong, certainly not the noble and gracious Prince Charming of the tour of Australia and the corroboree at Cook where he received her, her fourth-generation royal curtsy for his princely gift of pipes and tobacco and blankets flashed round the world by "cinema-scope" . . . the photograph she treasured—"Edward P."

Not he! It was a Russian or a Prussian plot, she firmly believed.

"Be silent, please!" she reproved one of the Press girls. "How dare you repeat such ugly slander? I'll thank you never to mention His Majesty's name again in my hearing. Excuse me!" Cheeks pink, eyes flashing, she was gone.

I never knew her to raise her voice in anger. She relied on wide-eyed innocence and honeyed sarcasm, sometimes tart, or on a speechless stare of withering scorn. Pride and prejudice were her little venial sins, never hurtful, never sullen for long, but shying at shadows, highly sensitive, "lacking a skin". She sometimes mistrusted her dearest friends, thought they were patronizing or lacking in frankness. Sometimes she was too patronizing, too hoity-toity, for her friends.

In the early nineteen forties, while I was absent in Sydney in years of exacting work with travel, Daisy remained in Adelaide, dedicated and devoted, staying at the Queen Adelaide Club and later in a small suite at the Grosvenor Hotel. In a highly professional office in the city each day she was patiently at work, the Commonwealth Government and university senates provided the funds and furnishings for secretarial help. Two girl graduates were specially selected for clerical proficiency and keen interest in collating and compiling forty years and a couple of thousand ragged and dusty foolscap pages of miscellaneous knowledge and notes, scattered with Aboriginal words in any one of fifty languages, to be classified into subject, chapter and verse, page, column, footnotes, addenda, appendix, index in approved academic hieroglyph and formulae.

Betty Collins, Barbara Jones—to each a year of cryptograms and scrabbles of unpronounceable words that might be all consonants or vowels—theirs was the job of "dollying" and "penning out" Daisy's anthropological "ore at grass". She had given the years of her strength to digging it out while there was time. She could explain, expound, expatiate, translate, knowing it all by heart, but she hadn't a hope of transcribing alone and nobody else in the world could do it when she was gone. Theirs was the heavy work of tracking up traces and indications, of finding, sorting, filing, referring, finalizing for coherence and continuity. They set together the jigsaw, all facets of Aboriginal life in the written word for readers and writers and students a century on. It was a long and exacting task, but now the little swag of it, one woman's gatherings saved from oblivion, is shared by national archives and libraries.

Ninety-four folios, in triplicate, were signed, sealed and delivered to the Commonwealth Government when I met her in Sydney, staying at the Queen's Club en route to be a guest at Federal Government House and receive what she called her "honorarium". They had asked her to suggest a sum of money to cover her part in the work—this was apart from other expenses and the salaries paid. She was to value the invaluable.

"£400?" she asked me several times. "Would I appear grasping if I asked for £400? Would I be a 'daughter of the horse leech'?"

Of the value of real estate in the Stone Age I had no idea, but "Why not £500?" I asked her.

Fingertips together, head on one side and a wide-eyed admission of guilt, she said, "Because I owe one of the big stores £400 for sending up groceries and clothes and sweets and all to my natives the last two years. . . ." So it would all go.

For all the fire of loyalty—"My country, right or wrong!" —she hated and abominated war, as a homicidal delirium of

L

the nations, a Moloch devouring the minds and bodies of men, a world shame. She was all patriotism, naturally, but in grief and longing for peace. Her war-work was whole-hearted but eratic. She was out of place in the regimental teams of service women—undomestic as knitter of socks and maker of cakes and diffident as a street collector rattling a box to ask for money. She would rather fill her own with coins than accost people. The war news, the marching armies and the blare of military bands, the black-outs and the ship-loads of refugees, distressed her, and the austerities of the coupon books. She never could manage the "giggly-winks" of coupons and gave hers away, to find that no longer could she be sure of her only enjoyment and stimulus in frequent cups of tea. Sadder still were the needs of her natives, their coupons controlled and commandeered by the white people in charge of them, and now none of the little hand-outs and hampers of clothes, meat, sweets, and for them, too, the comfort of a billy of tea. War or no war, she made up her mind to go back to them . . . but even the war had its smiles and surprises.

Packing for tent life in the wilderness, she came to me with a trim little suitcase filled with what she called her under-linen, don't you know? Worn to transparency and going grey, it was nearly as old as she, surviving the desert waters and the desert trails. She had renewed it lately, she explained, for the years of her second hegira, you see, but once upon a time it was the best of Irish linen and too good to throw away. She had had it laundered and mended beautifully, and offered it to the Red Cross in Adelaide. Some poor souls would surely be glad of it in concentration camps, or refugees.

She held some of the bundles up for me to see—a wasp-waist corset branded "Sibyl" in large gold letters indelibly with twenty-three loop-over clips of steel in front and lashed with cross-cords at the back like the rat-lines of a ship, Jaegers bought in Perth at the turn of the century, hard as a board and shrunk to the size of children's wear, cami-knickers and combinations with frills below the knee, neck-wear whaleboned under the ears, "ladies' flannelette nights" chin to toe, ribbon-threaded camisole, chin to brisket, to be battened down with twenty hooks and eyes . . . they were nearly all tissue-paper thin, "see-throughs" long before their time.

"The Red Cross didn't seem very pleased to have them," Daisy said, "so I thought I might try the Free French." There was a twinkle in her smile. I suggested the Historical Society Museum.

Where are the little tailored suits, I wonder—age could not wither them, nor moth and rust consume—and King George's umbrella, her life-long shade and pride? She asked me to take her picture in each and every one of them, using colour-photography films and slides, which I joyously did, including the evening frock, in a mannequin parade of one at Streaky Bay five years before she died. She was bright and graceful, a quick-change artist as dainty and photogenic as any model, at eighty-seven years old. We both wanted the pictures for library record, but the two spools were never returned from the colour-developers and receipt was denied though registration was proved.

Her last treasured possession, the exquisite seventeenth century miniature of an ancestress painted in France, the family heirloom she wished to send to Violet, was stolen in Adelaide. On the post office corner she was discoursing to some Pulteney Grammar schoolboys in her wonted way about her natives when a youth on a bicycle cruised in to the kerb and snatched her bag. In it were only a few shillings

163

and the cherished miniature, too precious to leave at the hotel, precious to the family for four hundred years.

Never a collector, she had given away her few Aboriginal relics, but there were some death-bones of grisly history, letter-sticks and a few of the sacred boards, *churinga* and *wanningi*, a few of the ritual man-making and murder knives, bones, stones, charms, of unusual interest, shields and boomerangs elaborately carved, spearheads of beryl and rock-crystal serrated like rose-leaves, a Stone Age surgeon's stock in trade and man's first tools. She sent some, with data, to friends in England, some to museums.

"What did you do with your *bambooroo*?" I asked her, of her magic-stick of interest to archaeologists, once written up by one of them in the London *Times*.

"*Yanda ngoonin inyillee!*" she reminded me, "Sun sitting down inside. I've kept that for you, because you're my spiritual child, don't you know?"

So I have her *bambooroo* here beside me, and it is one of the reasons I have written this little book about her when those who remember her as she was in life are very few.

After the ninety-four folios, she went back to the tent in the bush to be again the Woman Who Lives with the Blacks, but she couldn't find them. Across Eyre Peninsula to the shores of the Bight it was a long way for an old lady to go, and brave to take up the dedicated life. But at Yalata near Fowler's Bay, at Wandunya Water, at Yuria Water and Yooldil-gabbi, all her natives were gone. From every siding of the Transcontinental line the string of beggars in rags lazily waving the flies out of their eyes, selling the brummagem boomerangs daubed with wattle-dots and koala bears, was gone. A few withered wurleys and the white ashes of their campfires were still there.

In the legislations and regulations of World War II all

over the continent they were mustered and moved to the nearest missions and compounds. Some went into the services, Army, Allied Works Council, C.C.C., man-powered with tens of thousands to build Army installations, roads and bridges, from the Arafura Sea to the south. Some travelled in cattle-trucks two thousand miles to colonies on the outskirts of cities and towns, to be employed in priority industries and factories, the children at native schools, and all under control and curfew rules. For their own protection they were hurried out of sight "for the duration" and long after that. A blending of all the tribes, languages mixed together and forgotten in favour of English, the children brought up with no knowledge of Aboriginal crafts, laws, customs, was the general and inevitable result.

They were well fed, instead of hunting and foraging for themselves. They were decently clothed, some in uniforms, which they loved. Their physique, strength, energy, rapidly improved. From association in equality with the white people their ambition, acquisition, emulation and comprehension of twentieth century living settled them down in the new environment with no memory of the old.

After the war, those who returned to their own countries would not revert to the nomad life of fathers and mothers ten thousand years out of step with the modern world. In a spectacular success of education and adaptability they have asked and received the liberty to vote and to drink alcohol, fraternity in freedom from the curse of colour-line, and equality instead of slavery in the award wage, the conditions of employment and the State their good provider in youth and age . . . but they have lost their country and their Dreaming. Silent are all the hills and valleys of the lands they loved and their shadows are gone. Their orphan waters will never see them again. They have taken the white people's names and forgotten their own.

To sing and dance corroboree, to throw a come-back boomerang, to paint on bark and to blow the *didgeridoo* and, more important, to understand the symbols, totems, ceremonies, and legends: these they may now learn in "social studies" at school. Their forbears and the life they lived have vanished.

Their Kabbarli, returning from the shores of the Bight, travelled eastward in search of them along the Murray River, where at Loxton she set up her tent between two trees in a curve below the red cliffs and waited patiently for them to appear. In eight or nine months none of them arrived. Most of the Murray River full-blood tribes were extinct in 1885. The Dark People were seen now and again, wandering up and down from their little colony of motley on the Victorian side of Robinvale. Three or four generations from tribal days and ways, they worked in the vineyards and orange-groves as pickers and packers and listened to radios, bet on the races, went to the movies and led their own lives. Not one of the Old People could be found, dead or alive, so back she came to Adelaide in 1945, but restless, to leave again for Streaky Bay, on the edge of the Great Australian Bight, in the following year. Her letters had found me in the far north of Australia in the wreck and ruin of Darwin just after the war, and the Adelaide River Army camps, down through the Kimberleys and goldfields to Perth, and across by the new Eyre Highway to Melbourne in 1947.

Tent life on the Murray River flats a mile or two from the town with the nearest neighbour half a mile away had been a long and difficult sojourn, valiant but very lonely. The rigours of tent life were beyond her now. She told me of various kindly women, some of them trained nurses, who had induced her to share their homes in order to take care of her, but they became too solicitous and she refused to be taken care of. For the first time in hospital at eighty-seven years old—and then only for a few days—in a clash of wills with the matron she promptly packed and departed the place in dudgeon, consulted a city estate agent, and rented a seaside house in the suburb of Henley Beach in Adelaide. That was impractical, for she couldn't cook and couldn't afford a housekeeper, so she wisely returned for the winter to Streaky Bay, a guest at the pleasant little hotel there when I called to stay with her for a week as I was passing by. She was overjoyed for a very good reason.

Dreams of another book were in her mind, a collection of legends and blackfellow fables and fairytales to be dedicated to the Royal Highnesses Princesses Elizabeth and Margaret and their children, the heirs-apparent . . . always provided they would most graciously permit and accept the dedication of one who by five generations of their royal family had been inspired and sustained throughout the days of her life.

The Commonwealth had reserved and presented to her one copy of the ninety-four folios of data, with copyright for her use of them during her lifetime. She longed to see a volume complete of the legends especially for children of the Empire, wanted it published before she died. They were all in the rough, some in many versions of different tribes. She herself had tried and tried to collect and re-write for publication, for illustration, but she had failed and no ghost of a writer or editor could she find. Would I undertake it, or would I work with her again?

I was then deep in the history of Darwin and the Northern Territory, I explained. She was very disappointed. Learning that I would return to the West, she longed to come with

167

me, to follow her campfires on the old trails. Nothing would make her happier, she said.

In Mebourne I bought a caravan, quite new, roomy and bright for her to travel in comfort across the Nullarbor Plain and the wilderness of the central-west to Broome. On my return to Streaky Bay she had left the hotel to stay at the barley farm of Mr and Mrs Matthews, miles from the town and with her, arranging board and residence, I stayed for three weeks. But when the departure for the West was discussed I was informed by residents of Streaky Bay that the Department of the Interior at Canberra had taken over the responsibility for her well-being in her great age, now frail and needing constant care, and that a relative of her family, named Brownrigg, lived somewhere near and was in touch with her. This overruled the caravan journey. Neither of us mentiond it again. I was sorry later, for the information was not true. There was no authority or reason to keep her in South Australia. She was to live for four more years, still and ever alone.

Nicely cared for at Streaky Bay by Mrs Matthews and family, she romped with the children, talked with me of her childhood and her natives as we walked in the fields of barley by the windy bay. It was a modest little farm in a marginal area where the settlers were re-planting the salt-bush over the withered wheatfields where the dry wind had blown the soil away. Daisy had chosen the district because she was quite sure the natives from the missions about would come back to Yalata, not far away. Their descendants are now to be seen there in an unusually happy and independent little colony at the present day.

At night I would sit on the edge of her bed in the darkness while from a photographic memory she lived the past again, in her low tones and dreamy as though reading verse—the wistful years in Ireland . . . the little girl singing "Frère Jacques" and dancing in the Luxembourg Gardens . . . her coming-out dress in London . . . Tasmania and its friends of merry memories, and the rollicking life of western New South Wales in the days of the blade shearers. But mostly she spoke of the natives, the noble generous men and women who were her friends and worthy of her trust, estimable characters and as lovable as those of any other race.

One night I remember a sudden fright of "something burning". Spirals of blue smoke ascending from the end of her bed cut short the reminiscences in a wild rush for smothering rugs and hoses putting out a rising flame, the whole house alarmed. Only Daisy was unconcerned. She had heated a brick for warmth in the old Irish way of it, as she had done through all the years where water-bottles were useless, the rubber soon perished and the water scarce. The brick, wrapped in a bit of blanket, had started a spark and a blaze. No panic. She was annoyed at being interrupted. . . . "Where was I?" she said. "Oh yes, Jajjala dying!" and to the reek of burnt wool she started her tale again. I think she had never in life been really afraid.

At Streaky Bay she gave into my keeping several large manila folders of raw material for the writing of the legends, of Broome, of the Bibbulmun, of south coast and central west, Eucla and Ooldea. I carried them with me to Western Australia, to Key Farm at Toodyay, a guest house in the country where I stayed for three or four months writing night and day. My own book of the Territory was due for the publishers, but in the urgency of Daisy's advanced age and our "gentleman's agreement" I devoted an equal time to hers. Mine, now, was the task of finding the various pieces and fitting the jigsaw together, tracking up Aboriginal words in her glossaries, enhancing the simple stories with just a touch of drama or poetry for appeal both to children and as general literature with anthropological verifications and value—a link in the world's mythologies that delighted me. I need not say I had no thought of asking either an acknowledgment, a share in royalties or an editor's fee, and Daisy well knew this.

The work was in sight of the end at Key Farm when a brusque note came from her to say a bookseller friend of hers in Adelaide was leaving for overseas, and would meet her publishers in London, John Murray and Co., who showed keen interest in the book of legends to follow *The Passing of the Aborigines*. Would I please forward this and return all relevant manuscripts and notes immediately?

In anguish by air mail I asked her for another few weeks and the book would be finished. I had selected and rewritten fifteen of the legends, would need but another three weeks to complete the copies for the publisher, with introduction, letter-press, themes for illustration, all as a labour of love to appear with my own book simultaneously.

I received a telegram sharp and brief, repeating the demand for manuscripts and notes to be sent to the bookseller immediately. So I promptly parcelled them up and registered them to Adelaide, as requested. This time, however—and until such a request might be made from her to me—I did not include by own typewritten versions of the legends, to be for the second time ignored in acknowledgment and now dismissed peremptorily. I heard no more for a long time about those legends . . . except that the files and folders had been left behind at the back of his shop by the bookseller in Adelaide as incomprehensible, inexplicable and unpublishable in any category.

It is a matter to me of deepest regret that I did not return to Adelaide to lighten and brighten the poor little one's last years. My own life was wearing and exacting, with endless writing in Sydney and Melbourne, seven thousand miles of travelling the goldfields of Western Australia, and another seven thousand of the sandy mazes of Cooper's Creek and the Georgina to Cooktown and the Great Barrier Reef. Two or three times, to my sad surprise, knowing her independence, her pride, a request came for a small sum of money to be repaid. It was promptly sent, only £10 on two or three occasions, not worth mentioning, by no means adequate. The Commonwealth grant she received, on my representations, had twice been increased, but with rising costs was not enough for her economical living and astronomical giving. She had given her life away.

I heard she was being cared for and believed that her many friends in Adelaide, in their kindness and companionship, would be sure of her well-being. The last years, I have recently learned, were heartbreak.

The lone little figure, still quaint, still proud, precise— the fading fashion-plate everywhere known but always alone —wandered King William Street, purposeful but a little vague as to localities.

"Thank you, indeed! How foolish of me! I'm losing my youth, don't you know?"

Giving had been the routine of her waking hours for so long that she could not live on without it. Each morning she followed the tracks to the parklands and gardens with a shopping bag of small hand-outs—pennies and sweets for the children, bread for the ducks, crumbs for the sparrows, threepences for ices for girls and boys going home from school, a cake bought at a stall for an old lady, maybe a handkerchief, or liniment for cramp, or "coughin' medicine" for the Old People's Homes at Magill. They were the city stand-ins for the tribes of half a continent. "Aborigines" of the cities and the slums she could never understand, and she never sought them out.

At the age of ninety she submitted in silence to entering a home where she was cared for and respected, courteously thankful but never happy, never her gay and vivacious self. Kindly visitors to the home carried her off to a grannie flat in their own garden at Brighton for a time, and provided her daily needs and care from her pension. Her spirits revived when friends and strangers came to see her, journalists and authors among them. She was always a good story—but how could she tell them of her life's loyalties, her pilgrimage—"*Me, that've been where I've been!*" One day they brought a tape-recorder and made a record of the beautiful voice, question and answer, but the tape had been lost when I tried to find it—it was too late for a message, too brief for a theme.

Her long life was a blessing to her, with all her faculties and free of illness—the reward of the life's work, she believed in her faith. "Ninety years without slumbering", she still arose in the dark of piccaninny daylight to make a cup of tea for herself. She dressed in the *tout ensembles* green with age and badly frayed but meticulously brushed and pressed. Rain or shine she hoisted the royal umbrella, her halo and shield for fifty years, a symbol, shelter and shade. Where is it now, with the pony coats, the basques, the toques and the nine-gored skirts of great grandmother's day? When she died, were they thrown away?

Too frail to fend for herself at ninety-two, she returned to the home at her own request, but reluctantly even so, rather than be a burden. She was submissive, grateful and gracious to the end. Her last words, as they tucked her in bed one night, they told me, were thanks to the matron and the girls for their kindly service of the day . . . then, no trouble to anybody, free of the grief of farewell, she slept the last hours of her life away.

It was virtually a State funeral in Adelaide, attended by leading parliamentarians, university professors, officers of societies geographical, historical, ethnological, and of all benefit societies, education authorities, missionary circles— honours and laurel wreaths, flowers, and in the Press of Australia and overseas her valedictories. A grandson attended the burial—out of the silence of many years one of her own children, her own family, and though he remained unidentified he must have been proud of her, hearing the eulogies. Had it been a day earlier she, too, would have been proud and happy.

A quiet and solemn little crowd of Aboriginal Australians gathered at the graveside, saying good-bye in the name of their antique race to a lifelong friend. She alone would have known their totem, language and tribe. She died on 18th April 1951. The grave in the North Road Anglican cemetery in the lee of the Adelaide hills is lovingly tended and covered with flowers each year for her birthday, 15th October.

I remember her telling me once she would wish to be buried with her *wanna*, digging-stick, and *pitchi*, wooden scoop, as a Woman of the Dreaming in her own home ground at Yooldil-gabbi or at Eucla, where she became the Keeper of the Totems in the Australian desert sands.

Fame she has earned, and immortality. I think she would be content to know that the Aboriginal people for whom she gave her life did not die forgotten, as she sadly foretold, but through eternities of endless change will remember their Kabbarli—her name, when the world was young, written in smoke on the sky.

JUN 20 1980

JUL 0 9 1980

DATE DUE   ECHEANCE

OCT 2 0 1994

NOV 0 1994

JAN 1 2 1995

LAURENTIAN UNIVERSITY

UNIVERSITE LAURENTIENNE